Distant Thunder: Recollections of Lodi Area Veterans

Dr. Jennifer Holden
Editor

Paul Kuehn
CAPT Bob Bechill, SC, USNR
Cyndy Green
Michael Godwin
Aaron Raby
Bryan Tortolani
Daniel Unger

Sponsored by a grant from:

Distant thunder : recollections of Lodi area veterans /
Robert David Bechill ... [et al.] ; Jennifer Holden, editor.-
- 1st ed.
      p. cm.
  ISBN 0-9667532-6-7
  1. Veterans--California--Lodi Region--Biography. 2. United
States--Armed Forces--Biography. 3. Lodi Region (Calif.)--
Biography. 4. Oral history--California--Lodi Region. I.
Bechill, Robert David, 1955- II. Holden, Jennifer.

  U52.D573 2004
  355'.0092'279455--dc22

2004021624

Blue Moon Press

Modesto, California

A Subsidiary of Blue Moon-Lee Press

BluMoonP @aol.com

Preface

Many people and events led to the creation of this book. It all began on Veterans Day, 1998. As the Community Promotions Coordinator for the City of Lodi, I coordinated a gathering of local veterans, community members, and business leaders to create a commemoration event at Emerson Park to celebrate Veterans Day. The event included public speeches, a blessing, and entertainment by the Lodi High Drum Corps, followed by a community picnic where the conversations among veterans turned to their sharing stories of their tours of duty. Many had never shared their stories because they were too painful or forgotten, but the environment was a comfortable one. This commemorative event began an annual community tradition of gathering to share stories and to honor veterans and their families for their service to our nation. As community support expanded and attendance doubled and tripled, it became the consensus of the public that something permanent should evolve from the pride and appreciation citizens felt for veterans who served to protect our freedom.

About this same time an opportunity presented itself – a fountain between Lodi City Hall and the Carnegie Forum Council Chambers was in disrepair; in fact, the fountain had been dedicated in 1968 to honor veterans of Lodi. With the approval of mayor and city manager, a small fountain was to be designed to replace the existing one, and the structure would be dedicated to all Veterans. If you have visited the Lodi All Veterans Plaza, you already know that the idea of a small fountain became a dream project, a plaza that stands as a magnificent display of our community's generosity, pride, and heart. The design was not small, simple, or inexpensive, with estimated costs exceeding one half million dollars, but a group of community volunteers committed to get it done, feeling passionately that it was a necessary and long overdue project. A non-profit foundation was soon created to coordinate the project and fundraising efforts: a group of volunteers composed of representatives from all military branches, as well as local business professionals. This motivated group is now known as the Lodi Area All Veterans Foundation.

In 1999, a year later, the Foundation created a flag made completely of flowers for the annual event, and afterwards draped it across the steps of City Hall so visitors could pay their respects and have their photo taken in front of the flag.

In the fall of 2000, the Foundation added a Veterans Day Parade to its annual celebration, which ended with a groundbreaking ceremony at the newly dedicated location of the Lodi Area All Veterans Plaza.

In May, 2002, the Lodi Area All Veterans Plaza was dedicated to all veterans past, present, and future. Some of their stories are published in this book depicting the sacrifices they made not only in servicing their country, but also in having to leave their families and loved ones behind.

Volunteers devoted their energy and countless hours working to create, plan, and construct the Plaza, with the founding board of directors leading the way. I would like to extend my appreciation to and acknowledge these dedicated individuals who were the founding board members; Timothy Fowler, Steve Jarrett, Chuck Higgs, Phil Felde, Pat Catanzarite, Phil Jolly, Mary Galvan, Tony Galvan, Francis Capone, Bob Lagomarsino, Charles Mauch, Bill Pfeifle, Brad Jones, Richard Carpino, and Carol Marvel. I would also like to recognize the following City officials who supported funding the Plaza: City Manager Dixon Flynn, Mayor Steve Mann, Council Members Susan Hitchcock, Keith Land, Alan Nakanishi, and Phil Pennino.

As word of the Plaza spread, I received many letters from veterans in Lodi and the surrounding community, sharing heartwarming stories about how the Plaza was a symbol of honor, and that erecting the memorial somehow lent them permission to be angry, cry, and heal their inner wounds until they were left with a peaceful pride and honor for their service. Many family members remembered stories they had long forgotten about difficulties at home while their loved ones served in the military. Several veterans recalled friends long forgotten, atrocities never spoken about, and what it was like to be so far from home and the comforts of their communities. These personal stories are what inspired the Foundation to create this book. Additionally, special thanks is extended to the Lodi Arts Commission for the provision of a financial grant which made this part of Lodi history storytelling possible.

The Foundation made a commitment to the City of Lodi to repay the $500,000 loan it extended to complete construction without delay in 2000. This Foundation continues to honor that commitment with quarterly payments, supported in part by the proceeds of projects such as the publication and selling of this book. The

Foundation's current Board of Directors are John Tudor, Carol Marvel, Sara Heberle, Pat Catanzarite, Timothy Fowler, Mary Galvan, Tony Galvan, Brad Jones, Bob Lagomarsino, Phil Lenser, Bill Pfeifle, Merle Warner, Bob Gross, Bob Bechill, and Cynthia Haynes. They continue their mission to fulfill this obligation with pride, honor, and creativity in support of the Plaza as it stands today and as it will stand forever.

If you have a desire to make a financial contribution you may go to our website for further information: http://lodiveteransplaza.org

Cynthia L. Haynes

Founder and Past President

Lodi Area All Veterans Plaza

Foreword

In February of this year, CAPT Robert Bechill of the United States Naval Reserves and President of the Lodi Area All Veterans Plaza Foundation approached San Joaquin Delta College with the proposal to interview veterans—and a few civilians—in the Lodi area, transcribe their stories, and gather them into a book. The result of that effort is *Distant Thunder: Recollections of Lodi Area Veterans*, a collection of stories and photos reflecting the experiences of forty-two veterans and one civilian from Acampo, Escalon, Linden, Lockeford, Lodi, and Stockton. Among the officers, enlisted, and draftees, nearly every branch of the military is represented: Air Force, Army, Army Air Corps, Marines, Merchant Marine, and Navy. The stories themselves vary in length and content, ranging from humorous and warmhearted to tragic and heart wrenching. However, all of the stories reflect the courage and commitment of young men and women who were called to duty and willingly served their country.

The writing team consisted of the following: San Joaquin Delta College students Michael Godwin, Bryan Tortolani, and Daniel Unger; C.S.U. Stanislaus student Aaron Raby; Middle College High School teacher Cyndy Green; San Joaquin Delta College administrator Paul Kuehn; and San Joaquin Delta College professor Jennifer Holden. The writers volunteered for a variety of reasons: their familial ties to the military, their desire to preserve our nation's history, their wish to bring Delta College closer to the community—to name a few.

Distant Thunder was an opportunity for the writers to spend hours with those whom they admire, respect, and honor, poring over photos and paraphernalia and thus reassuring the veterans that what they and others sacrificed for our country truly mattered. Unfortunately, the writing team was unable to interview all of the veterans who offered to share their experiences, and many wonderful stories did not get published in this volume.

Although the Division of Arts and Culture, City of Lodi awarded a grant to the Lodi Area All Veterans Plaza Foundation to write this book, the contributors volunteered their time, energy, and talent to its completion. In addition to the writers named above, project coordinator Robert Bechill and graphic designer Patty Wallace worked on a strictly volunteer basis, while Betsy Harvey of Blue Moon Press greatly reduced the publication fees. We are also indebted to final editor, Gwinnett M. Paden, 1st LT., WAC, WWII.

Many of the interviewed veterans denied being "heroes," insisting instead that only their lost comrades were heroes while they themselves were just doing their jobs. However, in the eyes of the project participants and the citizens of this country, *all* of our veterans are heroes. This book is an expression of our gratitude to those who gave of themselves so unselfishly in order to preserve our country's many freedoms.

We thank you.

Jennifer L. Holden, Ph.D.

San Joaquin Delta College

June 29, 2004

Distant Thunder Team
Left to Right
Bryan Tortolani, Paul Kuehn,
CAPT Bob Bechill,
Daniel Unger, Michael Godwin, Aaron Raby,
Dr. Jennifer Holden, and Cyndy Green

Contents

World War II

Korean War

Vietnam War

Persian Gulf War

Operation Restore Hope

Operation Iraqi Freedom

WORLD WAR II

Lt. Colonel Vincent Paul Anderson
B-24 "Liberator" Navigator: WWII
528th Bomber Squadron, 380th Heavy Bomb Group
Air Medal with Five Oak Leaf Clusters

Kiirun was a large coastal city on the northernmost part of the island of Formosa. This target was a 12-hour round trip from our base in Mindoro, Philippines. Our specific bombing objective that day was to hit the docks that the Japanese were using. We were carrying four 2,000-pound general purpose bombs. After directing the pilot to the target, and after we were on our final bomb run, I went back to the bomb bays and opened the bomb bay doors when the bombardier called for it. The bombs were released, and we scored an excellent hit on the dock area. When the bombs hit, they sounded like firecrackers going off. Our flight altitude was 20,000 feet, but even at that height, you could hear the bombs detonating. Pop! Pop! Pop!

Kenny Belknap, our bombardier, had done an excellent job with his bombsight, but there was only one problem. The flak had been heavy over the target, and we had been hit in the tail. Part of one of two vertical stabilizers on our plane had been shot away. It was very difficult to fly. Both the pilot and copilot had to get on the right rudder to keep the aircraft flying straight. Also, a severe vibration from the tail section had started. The whole crew got their parachutes on in case we had to bail out.

Our engineer, Technical Sergeant William "Willie" Watson, was an outstanding flight engineer. Everyone in the crew had the utmost confidence in Willie. He was always cool and collected and never seemed to be ruffled. He knew the B-24 like the back of his hand. In the past, when we had fire in an engine or when we lost hydraulic power and had to hand crank the landing gear prior to landing, I went and talked with Willie. After I saw that Willie was calm and confident and was sure that the necessary emergency procedures were being accomplished, I was always satisfied.

This day, with the tail shaking so badly it was hard to stand up, and with all of us in our parachutes on ready to bail out if need be, I again sought out Willie Watson. In contrast to the staid demeanor he usually exhibited, his face was red, his hair was messed up (what hair he had left, for he was balding), and he was sweating profusely. I asked him what he thought, and he said he had crawled back to the tail section to look at and it didn't look good. He thought that most of the tail could bust off at any moment and that we would probably have to bail out immediately. So, while I was not too worried before talking with Willie, now I was worried.

The long and short of it is that, after nearly a seven-hour return flight (the power was reduced to lessen the strain on the tail), we landed safely and without incident. Once the engines were stopped, everybody came out from base operations, etc., and

4

pictures were taken of the heavily damaged vertical stabilizer. One picture was taken of the pilot standing by the horizontal stabilizer, looking at the damage and scratching his head. They said they were going to send a copy of the picture to Consolidated (the B-24 manufacturer) with the caption, "The 380th Heavy Bomb Group Always Brings Them Home." Needless to say, we were all very thankful to make it back in one piece.

Editor's note: Written by the LT. Colonel Anderson.

Cpl. Stan Beckler
Army Air Corps: WWII
Marksmanship Medal

Listening to a symphony broadcast on the radio, I was quite upset that my program had been interrupted by a Presidential announcement. Every Sunday I would listen to the symphony broadcast and then Roosevelt gave a speech that would change American lives forever.

Pearl Harbor was a traumatic experience for the nation. A fever amongst young men sprung up to join the armed forces and defend the country. I was working in a defense plant before I enlisted. I worked on PB4-5A aircraft, which were used in spotting submarines. It was my job to clean out the inside of the gas tanks so they could be painted. I worked with 17 different solutions that were all bad for humans. My doctor told me to quit before I did some real damage to myself, so I got a job as a sheet metal assembler at another company. I was very concerned that Japan would attack the mainland U.S. I thought, "Dadgummit, I better do something about it." When I went to join the Marines, they told me to go away, so I joined the Army and went to Fort MacArthur in Los Angeles.

Aviation had always interested me, and the Army Air Corps was offering deals to guys like me who had experience. It was then I became an aircraft mechanic for the Army Air Corps. They gave me a choice of where I wanted to go, so I chose Luke Field in Arizona because I have always loved the desert.

When I was sent to boot camp, I had no close friends or family. I was 18, in a strange place, and it was my first time away from home. My feelings were such that I felt I wouldn't survive the war. However, worrying doesn't do a damn bit of good, so positive action had to be taken. To pass the time, I began writing music in the summer of 1943. It was a way to distract myself and get my mind off all my worries. Boot camp was not as rigorous as the

Ranger outfits or the Big Red One. We had a hell of a lot of calisthenics and marching with full packs. There wasn't a lot of obstacle course training partly because there was a big difference between my outfit and soldier outfits. My keeping a plane running was totally different from taking on a company of Germans who were shooting at you. There was Captain Reynolds, who was a very trim, handsome man. He trained us and ran ahead of us to set the pace, huffing and puffing the whole time. I was more interested in getting to work than exercising.

Soon after boot camp, I was shipped out to Yuma Airbase. There are two types of forces in the military: those that fight and advance against the enemy and those who train and supply those soldiers who are next into battle. Yuma was a training station for pilots and gunners of the 951st Training Squadron. They flew AT-6's, which had a Harvard single engine and two seats. My job was to service the planes and keep them in the air. I would get out on the field at around 5:00 am to prep and check the planes for flight that day. We later were given AT-17's, which prepared pilots for bigger planes and more advanced training.

A lot of crazy things happened at Yuma. While I was on a cigarette break, two B-24's were coming at each other and collided in mid-air. A B-26 pilot loved cactus and decided to dive bomb some cacti. He hit them, spraying cactus all throughout the plane. Some B-17 pilots would fly so close to the ground there would be sand in the gunner's bay. One of the pilots asked me to ride along on a flight from Yuma to El Paso. I decided not to and went to get a beer. Later, I saw a flash of light in the east. The plane had hit a mountain on the way back from El Paso. We had a kid airing up a tire, and the tire blew, taking his whole face off.

I found war to either bring out the worst or the best in people. One of my colleagues, who was an objector, went to fight anyway and died in Saipan. War brings out a person's true character. A person will either succeed or fail based on who they are.

M.M. Mate 2nd Class Petty Officer Joseph Blanke
90th USN CB: WWII
Sharpshooter Medal, Victory Medal

Joe Blanke: Norfolk, Virginia—1943

I enlisted for a two-year tour of duty. I was shipped out to the Hawaiian Islands from Virginia. My job included various tasks and required a wide range of skills. Some days I unloaded ammunition and other supplies, such as heavy construction equipment from ships. We built buildings; painted hospitals, built landing ramps for the Marines, dug trenches to bury the dead, and even built bridges. Many times after completing a building, a Japanese plane would fly over and bomb it, leaving us to start the project all over again. At times it was frustrating and dangerous work because many times we had to work under cover of night.

On one occasion I was on Iwo Jima, unloading barrels of fuel late at night, when I heard a strange sound. I wondered what it was. I then realized it was the sound of bullets hitting metal. The bullets were about fifty feet short of hitting the fuel cans. Everyone ran for cover. The sniper must have been just out of range. I thanked God for watching over us so many times; I didn't think I would make it home alive.

As I was a few years older than some of the other fellows, many of them looked up to me for strength and guidance. I feel like I was just doing my duty the best way I knew how.

Sgt. Earle E. Ennis

803 Engineers, Headquarters Company: WWII
P.O.W. – Philippines and Japan
P.O.W. Medal, Bronze Star

Earle Ennis: P.O.W. ID

I enlisted after finishing my second year of junior college. In those days it was called Stockton

Junior College; now it's Delta Community College. I figured that I was going to be drafted, so I decided to be smart and join. I enlisted on March 7, 1941, joining the U.S. Army Engineers. They asked me if I wanted to go to the Philippines or to Panama, so I said I'd go to the Philippines. My thinking was that instead of going to Europe where the war was, I'd go to the Philippines where it would be quiet and peaceful. I got on the ship to Manila on April 21, 1941, and when we got there they said they needed someone in the Coast Guard Artillery, so I said, "Okay, put me in the Coast Guard Artillery."

Two days later, they said they needed some engineers with some college training, so I said, "Okay, I'll take that." So, actually, I got into the United States Engineering Department Detachment. It had all the engineering supplies for the Islands; we had the warehouse in Manila where I was stationed. And there I was!

From that point on we were under constant bombardment from the Japanese. It was my job to take the supplies out to the various areas of the Philippines with a truck. I had Philippinos working for me. We would hire the local guys to do all this stuff, so I didn't have to do anything but drive the truck. We were being shot at all the time. During the war there was no entertainment in Manila because we were on the front lines. Our version of entertainment was to try to keep away from the planes and the artillery. We played hide and go seek with them—mostly hide.

When the war started, we were confined to Bataan and Corregidor. Corregidor had some stockpiles of food but not a lot. So we had to start cutting down. We were on rations in order to make the food last. We didn't know how long we were going to last, so we kept saying, "We're going to have more food rations coming" every day, but they didn't come. When the Japanese captured us on April 7, 1942, we were already hungry, and after that it was nothing but starvation and hunger.

The day after our capture, we began the

march to Bataan. The Japanese wanted to secure that part of Bataan because they wanted to fire their big guns at Corregidor, so they got us out of there fast. For me, the death march wasn't too bad. I had been there since the war started, so I was acclimated to the climate. A lot of the guys had just gotten there, and the humidity in the tropics was just terrible—it caused dehydration. These new guys would drink anything they could get their hands on. They drank water from ditches, and of course they would die. They got terrible dysentery.

Before the new recruits got there, we had quinine pills to prevent malaria and mosquito netting. I never got malaria but I got Dengue' Fever, which is another type of intestinal bug. It doesn't have the malaria in it; it is not quite as bad. I suffered from high fever for a while then I was fine. It was not like malaria, which came back all the time. We all got dysentery which was terrible. Beriberi was another disease that we suffered from. It was from a lack of vitamin B-1. Everybody got

Beriberi to some degree. There were two kinds. There was the dry kind, which just made you very sick, and then there was the wet kind that made you swell up like a balloon. There were guys with Beriberi that didn't make it. Here they thought they were going home, but they died. Mental attitude had a lot to do with it.

They only chained us when we were in an enclosed type of area or to take pictures—the Japanese were big on propaganda. We weren't chained together on the march; we didn't need to be. We were hungry and tired and they had the guns. The march was about sixty miles, but it took a long time to get there, about eight days. We slept at night in an enclosed area, so the guards could keep an eye on us. If we were lucky, about every two or three days, they would feed us something. I didn't see anybody get killed, but some guys said that they did see some killing. I was probably in the best part of the area of the march.

I got shot at a couple of times because I

would go out in the fields to get some sugar cane. The Japanese were lousy shots—thank goodness! I don't know if they were really trying to hit us or just scare us back into line. We wanted that sugar cane because it gave us energy, but they didn't want us getting out of line. When I enlisted in the service I weighed 160 pounds. By the time my ordeal was over, I weighed 97 pounds.

We were first taken to Camp O'Donnell, and then two weeks later I was put on the Northern Luzon burial work detail. We dug the holes or we took the bodies out and buried them. It got up to where we were putting about fifty bodies in a hole. We buried our own and the Philippinos too.

For the first six months in the Philippines, we stayed in the camps and had a lot of work detail. I later realized that the work detail saved my neck because the Japanese army had a hospital and I was able to work there. When we ran out of shoes, I was able to get some there, so that helped. I got in better shape and was able to go to town to get food—the natives would slip us stuff.

On November 4, 1942, the Japanese put us on a prison ship and we sailed to Japan. We were lucky to make it. The other prison ships were sunk by the U.S. because they weren't marked P.O.W. They put us in this big hull, where we tried to find somewhere to sit down. For toilets, they lowered a bucket. The area we were kept in on the ship was where they normally kept the horses when they were transporting their own troops. For twenty-one days we were cramped up in there. They fed us a little bit of food, which was also lowered down in a bucket.

The first camp we were taken to in Japan was Mitsushima (11/4/42-3/19/44). On March 20, 1944, we were taken to Kanose until we were liberated on September 5, 1945.

We were always hungry, starving, in the P.O.W. camps. All we talked about was food— never women or anything like that—always food, cooking. I kept a small diary where I wrote down some names of the other P.O.W.s and gathered favorite recipes from their memories of tasty dishes that their mothers or girl friends prepared. We would dream about the recipes. It gave us something positive to think about.

The main meals in the prisons were rice and soup. We ate anything else we could get hold of like roots, flowers, fish heads or guts—even pickled grasshoppers. The Japanese pickled everything unless it was fresh. One time they gave us tooth powder, but we didn't have any toothbrushes, so we put the tooth powder on the rice to make it taste good. We ate rice and soybean soup. Once they got a carload of blubber in, and we had blubber in the soup. It wasn't bad; it gave the soup taste.

My first work detail in Japan was working on a dam, building it by hand. The only machinery we had was a rock crusher. Everything else was just by hand. They beat us if we didn't work hard enough. We worked about ten to twelve hours a day. Every ten days we got one day off. We used that day to clean up camp and wash our clothes and that sort of thing if we could. We had our first bath since our capture in Japan. They had a communal bathing area. They wouldn't let the women come in with us, but we didn't care, we were just glad to get a bath. After the war, they were still working on the dam. I don't know if they ever got it finished!

The last year-and-a-half in Japan, I worked in a carbine factory. It is similar to a steel mill, with electric furnaces. Everyday we worked. We would get covered with dirt and dust, yet we were only allowed to bathe once a week, with no soap. The Japanese guards bathed every day.

They had seven big furnaces running in the carbine factory when we got there, and pretty soon they only had one left. We "fixed" them all up! We kept one going because in the winter, it was very cold there, and we would pour the carbine in these big pots. They let us take a pot into our barracks to help us keep warm. We busted up the furnaces with the long spades that we used to break up the carbine stuff. We would stick the spades in the furnaces and short them out. Then we would have to shut them down because if we didn't, they would have blown up. Once they were shut down, they had to be repaired, but the Japanese didn't have anything to repair them with. They didn't know that we had busted the furnaces on purpose. The Americans had the midnight shift, so they didn't figure out that we were responsible. We had a lot more time during our shift to accomplish our sabotage. We talked about what we would do if the guards caught us. They work in twos, so we figured we would just kill them and throw them in the fire so no one would know what happened to them. But we never did get caught. We assumed that we were slowing down the Japanese production of carbine by breaking the furnaces, but we didn't know if we were having any effect on the war. We just hoped that we were making a difference for the Allies.

We weren't provided with many clothes or shoes. We wore thongs. The Japanese didn't have any protective shoes over there. When we got hold of cloth, or when someone died, we would take their stuff and use it. We made socks and things like that. Some of us got burns on our feet. There were no doctors, but it didn't make any difference because there was no medicine. There were some medics among us, and they pulled one guy's tooth one time because it was abscessed. It was surprising when I got home; I only had a few cavities. They did furnish us with clothes that they took from the detainees. They gave us Eisenhower jackets, thank goodness, because it got really cold in the snow.

We had no hair because of the lice and the fleas. The fleas were so big they could pick you up and throw you over in your bed! The lice were all over the place. We couldn't kill them, couldn't control them, but we would sit down on our days off and pinch them in half.

We referred to the camps as "The Land of Diarrhea." There was no toilet paper. We each had a piece of cloth that we would wash out and use over and over.

I woke up one day and there were no guards, so I thought, "That's great!" Everyone was saying the war was over. This was after the drop of the second bomb. We were friends with the local natives, and they told us all the stuff that was going on. We knew about the dropping of the first bomb. The old folks had sympathy for us. The United States had helped them out when they had earthquakes, and they hadn't forgotten it. It was the younger Japanese who hated us. The older natives who told us about the bombing were scared. To us, the news about the bombing was great because the Japanese had told us that they were going to kill us if there was an invasion. We didn't really have an understanding of the magnitude of the bomb; we were just told that it was a really big bomb.

We went into town and tried to scrounge some food. It was just a little village in the mountains, so we had no problems with the natives.

Pretty soon a bunch of MPs came over to get us out of the saloon. We were told to get on a train. The U.S. forces hadn't known where we were; they didn't know of our particular camp. So they scrounged from some other camps nearby and got some food for us: sea rations and that kind of thing, which made us all sick, of course. We weren't used to such rich food. I tried, though!

After being liberated from the camp in Mitsushima, we flew to Okinawa in a beautiful B-52 transport. There were nurses there! We stayed in Okinawa for a little while and they gave us all new clothes, good food—all you wanted to eat. Then they put us on the ol' stinky B-24's and flew us to Manila. Actually, on the B-24 that I got on, there was an old friend of mine from Stockton, so I got to sit in front! I knew his brother, his father, and his family. They had a potato-salad factory in Stockton. I used to help them make the potato salad, so we were pretty close friends. It was nice to see someone from home.

We were then taken to a hospital in Manila, where we stayed for about a month. There was nothing to do in Manila because it was all blown apart, so we just stayed at the hospital. We could have as much food a day as we wanted—I just couldn't get full. The doctors would say, "When are you going to stop gaining weight?" And I said, "When I get full!" Every day we were given four cans of beer and two packs of cigarettes, one kind of pipe tobacco with a pipe, and three candy bars. I traded all my stuff for beer!

When the war was over, the FBI interrogated us. They captured the guards from the first prison camp we were in and put them on trial. All but two guards were sentenced to death by hanging. The other two were given life imprisonment. We had nicknames for these guards. There was one nice guy and all the rest were nasty. They weren't happy because they had been stuck guarding us instead of being able to go fight in the war.

We were real close because all we had was

each other. The first year I was prisoner number 22, then the next year I was number 36 because so many had died. I think the original number captured was 200, but eventually there were 100 in my group. We got to know each other very well. We haven't kept in great touch, but we have communicated through our local P.O.W. clubs.

Major Tony Galvan
Army: WWII, Korea
Bronze Star

I was motivated to protect my country, so I joined the Army out of college and enrolled in the ROTC program. Basic Training was in New Orleans, where I trained for the Pacific Theater rather than the European conflict. Alligators and snakes were my biggest enemies. We trained for the environment that we would encounter when we were to engage the Japanese forces during WWII. Learning to fire the rifles from trees and crawling through swamps in the worst humidity I had ever experienced was our daily routine. We could never get dry. We learned attack and evasion techniques. The only thing that got us through was guts. Boot Camp prepares a soldier to not only defend his country but also the men around him.

On the last day of training, I found out we were going to Europe instead of the Pacific. I arrived in France on Omaha Beach after the D-Day Invasion. The beach was littered with troop transports, and the bay was clogged with supply ships. I wasn't part of the landings of D-Day, but I have a deep respect for the men who gave their lives that day. It wasn't until two weeks later that I experienced my first combat in France.

The memory of crossing the Rhine River on pontoons sticks out in my mind the most out of all of my time in Europe. The ingenuity and sheer scale of the operation was a pure example of American soldiers at their best.

I built a lot of close friendships during the war. Soldiers and officers became family, and they took care of one another. The entertainers that came to lift the troops' spirits and give hope to the hopeless served their country just as did the foot soldier.

The war was horrible, and soon after WWII I found myself in familiar territory. At the outbreak of the Korean War, I was once again called on by my country, and my training in Louisiana helped me survive. It was during this time that I received the Bronze Star for my efforts to stop Communism. Without my fellow troops, I would not be standing here today.

In 1955 I married my lifetime love Mary, with whom I had corresponded frequently, and we built a relationship that has withstood the test of time.

Capt. Mary Galvan
Army Nurse: WWII, Korea
Army Commendation Medal

I enlisted in the Red Cross because of the need for nurses in the Army. I was shocked at the declaration of war in Europe because I had visions of getting out. I was very nervous in my first days of service and wasn't used to the leadership role I had obtained. I was assigned to go to Europe, and on the way over became very seasick. I stayed in France through the duration of the war and treated many patients.

One night, a patient got extremely sick, and I called a doctor to take the patient to surgery. He had an emergency procedure and lived. We tried to keep up the morale of the wounded that came to the hospital. Men who were wounded would come into the hospital and need comfort and conversation. I was an ear and voice of compassion for those soldiers.

While in France, General Eisenhower came to the hospital to see the dentist, and I was able to meet him and shake his hand. I was also able to meet Mrs. Roosevelt, and what a thrill it was for me to meet such patriots!

In my free time, I was able to communicate to people through letters, and, even through a radio transmission, I was able to speak with my family while in Switzerland on leave. In France, the nurses would give chocolate, cigarettes, and soap to the townspeople for fresh eggs. The people we encountered were always accepting and happy that the Americans were in the fight.

At the end of the war, I was with all of the people celebrating and drinking champagne. The contagious excitement filled France. It was a war to end all wars, but soon after I found myself involved in yet another conflict. In the Korean War, I was a nurse stationed in Japan. I have received recognition from the governments of France and Japan for my contributions to the war effort.

Sara Heberle
USO Volunteer: WWII
Bismarck, North Dakota

Sara Heberle: Bismarck, North Dakota

At the beginning of WWII, I wanted to get into the Women's Army Corps Band. I wrote a letter and said that I could play the trumpet, trombone, and kettledrums, as I was a band instructor. I received a letter back that I had been accepted in the WAC. However, my sister, two years older than me, had already joined the WAC, so I felt that it was not fair to my mother for both of us to be gone. I then moved back to Bismarck and became a teacher at Bismarck High School.

The teachers and I decided to join a group to help the veterans as much as we could. We realized later that Bismarck was a crossing point for the many branches of the service. We set up a USO so the young men could have entertainment without having to go to a bar, especially the younger boys who had never been away from home before. They would have a place, a home away from home. The whole city kind of welcomed all the boys. Some people opened their homes so they could stay overnight.

We did three shows three times a week, especially on the weekends. We had soloists, and I did a few comedy routines. We would encourage the soldiers to join in group singing. We had a piano player who played by ear and could play any song in any key. There was a never-ending stream of soldiers coming through there.

We also formed a group that would go and meet the trains. The train always stopped for at least half an hour. We would hand out box lunches through the open windows to the soldiers who were not laying over. Some had a two-hour lay-over and would visit the USO. President Roosevelt also came through Bismarck on a train and spoke to us from the back of the train. It was exciting for all of us. I was selected to give him two dozen roses.

We had an army base there called Fort Lincoln. Some soldiers were stationed there. Once the war started, they moved out the soldiers from Fort Lincoln, and it became an internment camp for the Japanese. In fact, one of the beauty operators here in Lodi was someone I met there when we went to entertain that group as well. She was interned as an interpreter and her son was in my kindergarten class here in Lodi. What a surprise it was when she came for a parent conference!

My father owned a grocery store, and my mother was running the store because my father had passed away. She would put up many, many boxes of goodies. She put Spam, Vienna Sausages, canned fruit, and other things in the packages. We were sending out about ten packages a week to our friends and soldiers who were from Bismarck.

My father fought in World War I. The American Legion was formed in France during WWI. Bismarck, North Dakota, had American Legion Post #1. Lodi is Post #22.

Chief Petty Officer Charles Jessup
U.S. Navy: WWII

In 1943, before enlisting in the Navy, I had gotten a job to go to Greenland and be a plumber aboard a ship. I was leaving for Greenland soon, shipping out of New York by way of Sydney, Nova Scotia. Before shipping out, my mother and sister had asked me to drive them to Beacon, New York, to have their fortune told. It was only about a 25-mile drive. When I pulled up in front of the house to let them out, I told them I'd go to a nearby beer joint down the block and they could meet me there when they were finished. After several beers, I decided to see what was taking them so long. When I pulled up in front of the house, my sister came out and said I needed to go in and have my fortune told. I didn't believe in that stuff but finally agreed to go in just to speed things up.

The fortune-teller told me I had just come a long way from Newfoundland. I figured my mother or sister had told her that already. She then told me that I was going to begin a new job and make more money than I had ever made in my life. She said, "I can see you now. You are out in the ocean, rowing a boat and you are swearing at things flying overhead." I told her that she didn't know me very well because you'd never get me out in the ocean in a rowboat, and what would I be swearing at birds for?

After returning, I reported to my new job. It was aboard the S.S. Chatom, a luxury liner that had been taken over by the government during the war. We lay in the harbor for three days before shoving off. The fourth day we shoved off and steamed all day and all night. The next morning, right after breakfast, my roommate Slim and I were walking around the deck, amidships, when a submarine shot a torpedo and hit our engine room just below us. The concussion drove me back against the bulkhead. I could see the lifeboat in front of me was shattered. One man was blown up to the rail, hung there for a few seconds, and then dropped into the sea.

Slim and I had been assigned to lifeboat number 5. I said to Slim, "We better get topside and see if our lifeboat is still there." We laid up to the next deck. Our boat was still there with about 50 men standing in her. She was pretty rusted in her cradle. I said, "Hell, this ship isn't going to sink" and went aft to the fantail. There was a man there from my hometown. We talked for a few minutes then threw a life raft over the side for the men in the water. I told him we had better save a raft for ourselves.

At that moment, he climbed the rail and said, "So long, kid," and jumped into the water. There was only one raft left, and I threw it to him. Now the ship was lying over on its starboard side. I went back to my assigned lifeboat. The men were still standing in it. They couldn't get it out of the cradle because of the rust. I told them there were enough of them to carry the boat. So they all got out of the boat and we began shaking and moving it back and forth. Finally, it broke loose.

We walked it down the to the water's edge on the port side and shoved it off from the ship. I went back to get some parkas for the men and then we shoved off. When we were about 50 yards from the ship, she was down by the bow and the stern was in the air. The screws were exposed and all of a sudden, there was no more ship! We heard an explosion, and then we were all alone in the ocean.

Between Newfoundland and Labrador to the West, it looked like land. (Later we found out it was just a cloud formation.) The sea was fairly heavy with four- to six-foot waves. I stopped rowing after awhile and looked up in the air. I saw some four-engine seaplanes circling over us, looking for the sub. All of a sudden it came to me. Here I was in the middle of the ocean, rowing a boat and swearing at the planes overhead because they didn't land and pick us up, just like the fortune-teller said!

Lloyd Joachim

15th Engineers, 9th Infantry: WWII European African Middle Eastern Campaign Medal

Lloyd Joachim and wife, Esther: 1946

My eyes were so bad the Army gave me limited service for the first year. At the end of my first year of duty, I conveniently underwent an emergency appendectomy operation, which saved my life in more ways than one because it kept me out of the initial D-Day invasion. At that time, I

42

was still in the states, awaiting transport to England.

Once we arrived in England, I went across the Channel as a replacement. Replacements don't go in as a unit but are just thrown in wherever they are needed. I took the same path up Omaha Beach as those depicted in the movie *Saving Private Ryan*, but by the time I got there the beach was deserted. I saw all the junk left from the battle and was so glad that I had not been there. Of course, I would have been there if it were not for my eyes and the convenient appendectomy.

Once we arrived, we followed the road up from Omaha Beach and we eventually met up with the transport trucks. They packed us into those trucks like canned asparagus. The trucks were so packed with soldiers we could hardly breathe. Eventually, we arrived at the trains, which took us across France to our final destination. When we arrived at our unit, it looked just like a great big forest except for the many soldiers' helmets poking out of foxholes.

By the time I got to the front lines, I was in Belgium. We were fighting in the Hurtgen Forest, which is where much of the Battle of the Bulge occurred. At that edge of the Hurtgen Forest, we encountered a big battle. My unit was brought back for a little relief. I was a replacement and just thrown to the wolves. At that point, I started to get into the war right quick.

From there we went to Ardennes, where we attempted to cross a few rivers. We made a few dry runs and in the process we engaged in a few minor battles. We finally got up to where the Battle of the Bulge occurred. My unit was stationed directly across from where the Krauts were positioned to come across en masse that night. Luckily, that afternoon we were suddenly pulled out of there just before the Germans came across.

I was over there for nearly two years, and I was scared the whole time. The only time the fear dissipated was during the harsh winters when we were freezing to death. Every once in a while, it got so cold I didn't give a damn whether or not I got shot because I was so cold. We were all so cold that many of us just didn't care. When we were on the front lines we never took our clothes off. We would take off our overshoes and overcoats and climb in our sacks—as we called our sleeping bags—but that's all we dared take off. We did that for weeks at a time, without being able to change clothes or even change socks. It got pretty hairy.

My primary job assignment was mine detection. We almost always attacked at daylight, very early in the morning. First, we would bombard them with a bunch of artillery and mortars, and then I would move in with my mine detector so a tank could follow and hope I didn't get shot in the process. Someone had to go in and find the mines so the tanks could get through. The infantry would be on one side of the road, lying down in ditches, while I would walk out front with my mine detector. In a situation like that, I was an open target. I was bloody naked out there on the road. Even if somebody was aiming at the tank behind me, they were more than likely going to hit me first. We picked up a lot of mines.

I was mostly searching for anti-tank mines, which don't go off from the weight of the man. So I wasn't worried about the mines. I was much more concerned about being shot. The enemy often laid in artillery fire as an attempt to thwart our attack. The artillery fire was particularly dangerous because if it hit a mine it would set off the mine or it could hit *me*. I was shot at directly by a German 88. I was walking down the road, and they laid two quickies in and of course you cannot get out of the road fast enough. Luckily, I found a foxhole and landed in it. I sat there for a while and then went tearing out of town to where my buddies were.

One afternoon, I was all alone out on the road, shoveling some dirt, when a Jeep came through loaded with four GIs. These four guys came sliding up to me as I was shoveling and they asked, "Where's the ammo dump?" Now, that's not a question you would normally ask an ordinary GI standing on the roadside. Not to mention there were *four* of them in that Jeep. All four had their submachine guns at the ready, and all four were immaculately dressed. I found this alarming, because soldiers coming from the front lines never looked alike and as a rule they were covered with dirt from head to foot. If those four men had been American GIs, their heavy machine guns would have been in their laps rather than at the ready. They were definitely Krauts coming up to spy on us.

I reported the incident to my captain, but I'm not sure whatever came of it. There were a lot of those guys around at that time, and that still sticks in my mind because they had German spies trying to find that ammunition dump. All I could think of was how easily they could have shot me.

My most memorable experience was when we crossed the Ludendorf Bridge at the city of Remagen, just after its capture. Thankfully, it was captured intact, and this allowed the Allies to get through Germany's last major defensive line, namely the Rhine River. My unit—the 15th Engineer Battalion, 9th Infantry Division—was one of the early units to cross the bridge. It was for this act that my unit received a Presidential Unit Citation.

Once we arrived at the bridge, some infantry and tanks had already crossed. I was standing on the tailgate of a truck. Just as we got to the end of the bridge, I noticed a small mountain with a railroad tunnel running through it. While taking in the scene, I heard an airplane coming closer, but I couldn't see it. As I scanned the mountaintop, an airplane appeared out of the haze. Its engines were roaring as it came tearing down on us. Just as he got close, he cut the engines off and glided straight for us. He had a bomb! I could see it clearly. Try as I might, I couldn't tell if it was a German or an American or what. I just kept watching and watching, but the plane had no markings on it.

Because of my position on the far end of the

bridge, he was headed right at me. The plane came so close to me that if the pilot had been a guy I knew I could easily have recognized him; he was that close. Then he dropped the bomb. Of course, the bank was on a steep incline, but in order for the detonator to go off, he needed the bomb to hit dead on. Fortunately, the angle was wrong, and it hit sideways and tumbled into the Rhine without detonating. He roared off as I stared after him. We had anti-aircraft guns in place, and suddenly they began to fire on him just as he roared off, but they were too late.

The next morning we went around the hill to the spot where the Krauts had been shooting at us the night before. There were a few mines at the top of the hill, and so they sent me in with my mine detector after laying in a bunch of artillery and mortars to soften up the enemy. It was my job to clear a wide enough path for the tanks to spearhead the assault. It's a pretty hazardous job. You're unarmed because you need both hands to wield the

49

heavy mine detector, as well as being bloody naked out on the road while walking ahead of your entire unit. I picked off a few mines as I slowly made my way over the hill overlooking the town.

As I came upon the town, I heard the familiar sound of a tank. I thought, "Well, if we've already got a tank down there, what am I doing out here?" I took another look and saw that it was a German tank. He was only a block off, and he was coming straight toward me. As he drew closer I said to myself, "The heck with you." I then threw down my mine detector and dove into a foxhole. Fortunately, the tank was more interested in getting out of town and saving itself rather than messing around with me.

The enemy got up and hid behind a hill for a while. Pretty soon they started in. I wasn't able to get back to my group because there were tracer bullets coming across, so I went in and joined the infantry. I stayed with them, and we settled in an abandoned house. The German tank had hidden itself behind a little rise. After a while he set his turrets across the top of the mound and started shooting the heck out of us guys in the house. We couldn't locate our artillery or mortars, which we desperately needed if we were to mount a counterattack. This gave the Krauts time to regroup and mount their counterattack.

We had guys in all the windows of the house with machine guns fighting off the Krauts as they battled their way back in, trying to catch us. To locate a target, you have an observer telling the artillery to shoot, say, twenty yards to the left and twenty yards right. When we finally found our artillery and zeroed in on the Krauts, they soon surrendered, but by this time fourteen hours had passed. Because I had not made it back to camp, I was missing, and so I was listed as "missing in action."

My sergeant received a report that they had a dead soldier down in the town where I was last seen. The sergeant put two and two together and figured it

51

was me. So early that night, about eight o'clock, here came my sergeant tromping in to take my body out. He came in the door and there I was. He said to me, "Ah gee, we thought you were a goner." So I wound up helping them carry what was "officially" thought to be my "body" back out to our line.

Lt. Colonel Wayne Kildall
Army: WWII, Korea, Vietnam
Bronze Star

I wanted to be a tail gunner in the Army Air Corps. However, I ended up being part of the ground crew, supplying parts for bombers and fighters during WWII. I joined the Army after listening to a band concert that played patriotic music. In boot camp, we drilled with wooden guns and sat in foxholes while our drill instructors pelted us with tear gas. I never fired a rifle until I was out of boot camp. About six to ten guys were lost in the first days of the war because of poor training. They couldn't hit the broad side of a barn with their rifles.

We were transported to England on the Queen Elizabeth—24,000 men, rotating shifts of 8,000 to the sleeping bunks. There was a lot of spare time, and when it was time to sleep, I spent most of it falling out of my hammock and climbing back in. The English soldiers ran a casino on board and caught a guy rolling with loaded dice on an $8,000 pot. They were going to throw him overboard but put him in the brig instead. Our Second Lieutenant wasn't too bright, and one night he scratched the paint off of one of the portholes to see out, and the light could be seen for miles. The portholes were painted so as not give our position away to submarines.

The Army stationed me in England to prepare for the D-Day invasion. I was part of a B-17 crew in the repair and supply division. The morning of the D-Day invasion, we couldn't see the sun because of all the planes flying overhead. After the invasion, a tail gunner named Snuffy Smith won the Congressional Medal of Honor for bringing his flak-tattered plane back, putting out two fires and landing the plane. While I was in London, I was visiting Westminster Abby when a buzz bomb went off near the church. A buzz bomb is an explosive that buzzes just before it hits its target. Later, I flew over Europe to see the damage and was amazed at the devastation. The sight would be the reason for me entering the chaplaincy.

During Korea, I was part of a combat engineer battalion as their chaplain. The battalion had to lay a bridge over a river known to have enemy resistance nearby. A soldier asked me to pray for a cloudy day. The fog rolled in, and we didn't have to lay a smoke screen. As soon as the bridge was finished, the fog rolled away into a sunny day.

In Korea, I was stationed with an artillery battalion. Every night around 9 o'clock, an enemy plane would fly over, drop flares, and check our position. We called him "Bed Check Charlie." The very next day mortars would come flying into our position to marked spots that the plane had zeroed in. We ask if we could shoot him down but were told it would give away our position. The next day, I asked if I could go have lunch with the front battalion and the major said I could if we weren't under fire. Fifteen minutes after I left, mortars killed my gun crew. I always wondered why I was spared. After Korea, I was stationed in Germany and then to San Francisco as part of the Sixth Army.

In Vietnam, I would perform services for the Green Berets on the Cambodian border. I would fly in on Christmas, bringing their mail, and perform a special short service. We never knew what to expect in that flying area. One Sunday night after the service, the MPs called me into town. There was a soldier in the red light district, holding a grenade, and he was ready to kill himself. He was in a long house where a few families lived, and there was a pregnant woman in the room. No one would listen to him, and he thought he was the father of the Vietnamese baby. I noticed that the window behind me was too small to jump through, so I had to talk this guy down. I also knew that Vietnamese women would trick GIs into marrying them so that they would brought to the U.S. He told me that he had been given the runaround by all of his superior officers about this situation and that this was his only solution. I told him he didn't want to kill anyone, especially his unborn child. He got emotional and handed over the grenade.

Afterwards, the prostitute said he was crazy, and the MPs wanted to interrogate the soldier. I picked him up from his cell the next morning and took him to breakfast, then to his unit. The soldier wasn't given a defense lawyer, so I acted as his attorney because none of them knew the details of the situation. In the end, the soldier was sent to rehabilitative assignment, and my church attendance went up because I got him off.

There was also a local school that was in need of money, and it only cost $25 a year for 25 children to get all they needed. The soldiers in my company all donated more than was needed for funds, and the school was able to survive. These men were true humanitarians and patriots. In a bloody war, they produced something good and lasting out of suffering and strife.

Sgt. Roy W. Kirsten
6th Mechanized Cavalry Recon. Squad: WWII
Purple Heart

Immediately after school, I was drafted. I was called up for the draft into the Army. After basic training, I was sent to Fort Riley, Kansas, where I was put into the cavalry. I had the option of horse or mechanized cavalry. I chose mechanized cavalry and was sent to mechanics school. About six months later, I was in Le Havre, France, where I was put into a replacement depot. This was after D-Day, so there were a lot of casualties and a need for a lot of replacements.

The first day, I was put into a tank and told to repair the gun turret. I had no idea how to repair a gun turret. I just looked at everything and scratched my head. Finally, the sergeant came over and asked me if it was fixed, and I said, "No, I have no idea how to fix it." The sergeant told me to go over and fix a flat tire on a 6x6 truck. Well, I jacked up the truck. The snow that covered the ground melted from the heat of the jack and the truck, and that sucker came down after I got the tire off. The same sergeant came over and asked me if the tire was fixed. Well, I said no, it wasn't fixed. He took me away from that job and told me, "Now you're a tank crewmen." My job was the loader. I loaded the gun when we needed to fire it.

The Army put a bunch of us on a truck and we went from outfit to outfit, dropping off two or three of us at a time. Finally, I got dropped off. I remember walking across this big field with a sergeant. As we walked across this field, I could see puffs of smoke where bullets from some sniper were hitting the ground. I looked at the sergeant, and he didn't blink an eye. So I didn't blink an eye. Besides, he was on the side where the bullets were coming from.

The next day our unit took off for the front. We would travel about five miles in a day, which by Army standards was fast. We would encounter some opposition once in a while; it was comforting to be in that tank and hear bullets just bouncing off us. For the most part, the Germans were in full retreat. As we approached the Rhine River, we started taking a lot of prisoners. There were times when we would stop at night and sleep, and we would be surrounded by hundreds and hundreds of German prisoners and have no idea whether they would attack us or not.

As we approached the town of Numont, France, we turned this one corner and a German 88 tank stood right in front of us. The next thing I knew we were hit. There is one thing tanks try to avoid and that's a tank vs. tank fight. That's a no-no. Tanks carry three types of shells: canister, high explosive, and armor piercing. We were hit with a high explosive shell, which put shrapnel in my hand, arm, and butt. Our driver got critically wounded. If that German 88 had fired armor piercing instead, that shell would have gone right through my tank and hit me right between the eyes.

I would have been one of the last casualties of the war. I was lucky the war ended about twenty days later.

I finally got enough points to go home. The Army offered me a promotion to First Sergeant if I would stay in the Army, but I wanted to go home. I was proud to serve and do my duty, but I don't think I would do it again.

Pfc. Jay C. Lane
32nd Infantry, 127th Division (Red Arrow):
WWII
2 Purple Hearts, C. I. B. Badge

We were one of the first divisions to land on Luzon, a little island in the Philippines. We headed up the Villa Verde Trail and tangled with a very tough Jap army. This is where I first got wounded. A hand grenade was thrown in my direction, and it went off. My hand took a lot of shrapnel, which hurt like hell. Even today, I still get little pieces of shrapnel popping out of my hand.

As we headed up the Villa Verde Trail, I remember one patrol where I crawled up a hill to see if there were any Japs around. As I got to the top, I parted some high grass to see if there were. The only thing I saw was the front end of a Jap machine gun about a foot in front of my face. I heard a click then nothing. Fortunately for me their gun jammed. The Japs turned tail and ran away.

A few weeks later and further up the trail, I came face to face with a Jap officer. I pulled out my .45 and shot as I ducked for cover. I got up and looked to see if I hit him, but he was gone. I followed a trail of blood and found him bleeding to death. Just then some other Jap threw a hand grenade at me, and my buddies yelled at me, "Grenade! Look out!" I jumped off a cliff and hit bottom about 10 feet down. That grenade didn't go off. As I lay there, another grenade landed right next to my head. I was lucky that grenade also did not go off.

Not being a big man, I was volunteered for what was called a "tunnel rat." These men went into tunnels to find Japs or other important things. The Japs had thousands of tunnels everywhere. I remember going into one tunnel with my .45. I looked around for awhile, found nothing, and came out. After I came out, I discovered that my .45 wasn't working. I guess it was a good thing I didn't find any Japs. The only thing I could have done was maybe throw my .45 at them.

Finally my luck ran out. Five days before the war ended, I ended up getting shot in the leg.

RDM 2nd Class Jack M. Little
U.S.S. Satterlee, U.S.S. Madison: WWII, Korea

"Greetings, Uncle Sam needs you." I received my induction notice for military service in 1942. Ironically, in 1941, just after Pearl Harbor, I went down to the Navy Recruitment Office and tried to enlist as a 17 year-old. The chief told me to "go home and grow up." Following my induction notice, I went back down to the Navy Center in Fresno, CA, and who was there? The same chief who told me I needed to grow up.

After completion of naval training, I was assigned to the destroyer U.S.S. Satterlee (DD 626). In the Navy I was a radarman where I operated and maintained the air, ground, and fire control radar. I was also trained in dead reckoning, which is used to plot contacts.

In July, 1943, we put out to sea. While in San Diego, Henry Fonda, the actor, joined the crew of the Satterlee. I remember as we approached the

Panama Canal, people lined the canal to get a look at Henry "Hank" Fonda. We finally headed to Boston Harbor to get outfitted with supplies and a full complement of sailors. We then headed down to Norfolk, Virginia.

On June 5, 1944, the night before D-Day, my ship left Portsmouth, England, as a lead ship. Our job was to escort troop ships across the channel. After that, everyone waited for H-Hour. There was some time to reminisce and wonder what combat was going to be like. There were a few sailors who had seen action, but most of the crew was just well trained kids.

When H-Hour came, just as the sun began to rise, the battleships and other ships opened fire. The firing was deafening, and the smell from the guns was very noxious. The German 88mm artillery began firing back. There were shells exploding on both sides of my ship. What usually happens next is a direct hit. We were lucky; we didn't get hit. We provided fire support until we were down to 15% of our ammunition, and then we were to return to Portsmouth, reload, and head back.

The Satterlee's replacement ship was blown into two pieces by 88mm shells. We returned and fired our guns until we were down to 5% of our ammunition. Another ship relieved us, and we returned to Portsmouth to re-supply. We were a very tired crew.

Pfc. Jack L. Molini

Company B, 363rd Infantry Division: WWII

Purple Heart, 2 Bronze Stars

Jack Molini: taken just before leaving the Army

My division entered the war in Italy. We started out our march in Naples and went up through Anzio, Rome, to the Arno, the north side of the Apennines Mountains, and ending up in the Po

Valley near Legnago. This was a hell of an experience for my buddies and me, but we made it. My company size averaged about 140 men. By the time we got to the Po Valley, 50 were killed in action, six more died of their wounds, and 39 were seriously wounded in action. Only a few of us made the entire journey without a scratch. The terrain was very tough. There were numerous mountain peaks, streams, deep valleys, and broken ridges. All this provided excellent defensible positions for the Germans. It was very hard to make any advancement on the Germans, but we did.

I remember this little village in the mountains called L'Uomo Morto (dead man). At the time I thought, "what a hell of a name," and was it giving us a warning of what was to come? One night on some mountain we had dug in, I had fallen asleep and was awakened by a noise. I looked up and there were white faces staring at me! For a second I didn't know what to do. Fortunately, it was only goats looking down at me. We almost had chops for dinner!

Throughout the entire winter months the ground was covered with snow two or three feet deep. We survived the best we could in our dugouts covered with sandbags, occasionally going on patrol at night. On one occasion on another damned hill, I heard something to my rear. I turned my head to see, and three German soldiers were not 20 feet behind me, armed; their rifles pointed in our direction! I motioned them forward and they dropped their arms and surrendered. We had lucked out again! They were as tired of fighting as we were.

On April 26, 1945, I was wounded at Legnago, Italy, after crossing the Adige River. The bullet entered my head below the bridge of the nose next to my right eye and lodged below my left ear. When I regained consciousness, two of my buddies, Charles Reese and Ben Warner, were dead next to me. I crawled about 200 feet and collapsed. I was really scared. Finally, someone found me, and I was taken to a first aid station and then to a field hospital. The doctors were amazed that I survived. Two days later the war ended.

Sgt. Harry Momi

350th Infantry Regiment, 77th Division: WWII
Purple Heart with Oak Leaf Cluster

Harry Momi: 1945

I'm originally from Stockton—born there and went into service from there. I'd never been away from home. I entered the service the first part of February, 1943. I was still in high school. You

72

know how young kids are—didn't care for school too much. "I'm going to join the Army," and that's what happened. I went to Fort Ord and then they sent us to Fort Brady, Michigan, which is on the border of Canada in a town called Sault St. Marie. I was there for six months and then was transferred to Fort Benning, Georgia. I was there for another five months of training, and then I was transferred into the 77th division in Camp Pickett, Virginia.

What made it nice is there were five of us from Stockton who stayed together. That made it a lot easier because we were compatible, as we were all from the same town and we knew each other before we went into the service. It just happened that way. There's three of us alive now; the fourth one was a fighter. His name was Tote Martinez. He died after the war. We came through the war alive.

We went from Camp Pickett to Hawaii. We spent approximately two months in Hawaii, and from there we went into battle. The first battle we were in was Guam. It was my first time in battle. I was scared out of my pants. Great American soldiers; they were brave, super guys who I was with, and they weren't afraid of nothing.

We landed at Agat on Guam. It's a long time ago; it was in 1944. I had been in the Army a year. We had to walk, I think, a quarter of a mile. There was so much coral in there that we couldn't get the boats in close. When we got out, the water was up to our waists. We weren't fired on when we landed. When we hit the beaches is when all hell broke loose. I don't know how many Japanese were killed. Our tanks came later. We had a hell of a time getting our tanks in there because of the coral.

Ie Shima: that's where Ernie Pyle was killed; that's the island that we fought on. And then we fought on Okinawa. See, this is the type of fighting that you do. When you fought the Japanese, a lot of them were in tunnels and caves, and you had to dig them out. We used flame-throwers. That was the only thing that worked. It's hard to explain; it was so long ago. It was a small island. Let me explain Ie Shima to you: a tiny island full of land mines. Full of land mines. There was one kid walking in front of me, and he stepped on one and it just disintegrated him.

My tank was on the road and we had stopped. We were supporting the ground troops and there was a lull. A couple of the guys were talking, and this gentleman came up all of a sudden—no arms or anything. We said, "Who's that?" They said, "That's Ernie Pyle." Holy smoke! So I went up to him and I said, "Hey, Ernie, what are the chances of getting your picture? I got a camera in my tank." He said, "Sure," and he got up on top of our tank, and I took a picture of him.

That's how I got to meet Ernie Pyle. I think it was about fifteen minutes later that he was killed. He was with one of my officers in a jeep, and all of a sudden fire started; the Japanese started shooting. They jumped out of the jeep and went on the side of the road into a little ravine. He got up to look around and see what was happening, and that's when he got killed.

I don't know a lot about him. I do know that he was a famous correspondent. I sent this picture to his wife after the war. I wrote her a letter and sent her this picture—that this was Ernie in his last hour, and so I just thought maybe she would like it.

Ernie Pyle on top of Harry Momi's tank: April 18, 1945

Chief Petty Officer Scotty Nilssen
U.S.S. Roosevelt, U.S.S. Midway: WWII
Presidential Unit Citation, Air Medal

Scotty Nilssen: Pearl Harbor—1941

I joined the Navy in February of 1940—
Valentine's Day. I had no reason; I just wanted the
Navy. With a few exceptions, all of us were about

eighteen or nineteen years old. It was two years before Pearl Harbor. I didn't know anything about war. I traveled from Tokyo to Istanbul, Turkey, when I was in the Navy. I was in what they call a flying boat squadron. It was a plane that had a hull that was like a ship—a flying boat—and we did patrol work. We would fly twelve hours a day looking for the enemy. That was basically what these planes were used for and for looking for submarines.

We would fly patrols up and down the Solomon Islands from about seven at night to about seven in the morning, looking for enemy ships, which we spotted periodically, and then we would radio back to land and the planes would know where to attack them. It was pretty brutal. We were at ten thousand feet and the tracers from the Japanese boats were going up past us. I don't know how high we would have had to get to get away from them . . . but luckily they missed us.

We'd sit in these airplanes for twelve hours.

Sometimes we'd hit bad weather; sometimes we'd hit good weather, and we'd just keep flying and flying and flying and luckily very few times did we ever sight a submarine or anything. That's what I mean by monotonous. At nighttime—half of our flights were at night—there was not a heck of a lot we could look for, maybe just a light here or there or gunfire from the water below us. The Japanese below were shooting at us. But we lucked out; they never hit us.

Pearl Harbor. I was there. I was at a Naval Air Station called Kaneohe, and the Japanese came in and hit Kaneohe first because it was in the line of flight. They came on one side and attacked us and then flew over the mountain range and went to Pearl Harbor and attacked there about three or four minutes later. We had a lot of casualties. Pretty brutal.

I was in a hangar, firing at the Japanese with a rifle that was made in WWI. That's the kind of equipment we had in those days. If I had a potato, I could have hit them—they were flying pretty low.

They did very little bombing. Most of the damage was from machine-gun fire. They were after the planes that were on the ground. We had thirty-three planes, and they destroyed all of them. Twelve of the planes were thirty days old. We had just picked them up brand new in San Diego, and they were all destroyed. It was a complete state of chaos—everything was burned. Hangars were burned.

Other men were doing the same thing I was— grabbing guns and shooting back as best they could. There were a lot of casualties . . . people with their heads blown off. Stuff like that.

I think I might have shot one down. I wasn't sure. All I know is one came by and we started shooting at him, and he went down into the ground. The only one we shot down. The whole thing lasted a couple of hours.

A second wave came behind the first one. When the first one ran out of ammunition and stuff, you know—gasoline—they launched another group of planes to come in and attack us, so they had two groups that attacked us.

I had no idea what had happened in Pearl Harbor until they sent me over there. I was sent over there the next day because we had no planes left to fly and Pearl Harbor still had some left over. I stayed there for a month, and I had to sleep in the hangar.

What did I feel at the time? All I remember is someone said they were the Japs and it kind of upset us a bit. We just grabbed whatever we could get hold of and started shooting back. That was about it. I was nineteen years old.

During Guadalcanal, I got treated for tropical diseases. I had malaria, dengue fever—all kinds of other miserable diseases. They put us in an old tent. I went down to ninety pounds. My normal weight was 150. It was pretty tough—malaria, dengue fever, dysentery, and stuff. It was too much for one person to have. I had it for a couple of months, but the malaria stayed with me for years. After I came back to the states, I got these malaria attacks. It was kind of like the flu or something—hot and sweaty and feeling miserable. I'd lie down and the next day I'd begin to feel ok.

The President gave a citation to our squadron for work that we did in the Pacific area. It was for outstanding service that we performed. We attacked the enemy, and we held them at bay. That was the first time that the Japanese were unable to advance. That was the first time they were kicked back in the history of their nation. That's what we got the citation for.

Seaman 2nd Class Ocie Norton
U.S.S. Forrester: WWII

I was assigned to the U.S.S. Forrester, which was a destroyer/minesweeper out of Boston. The ship was armed with three five-inch guns, four forties on each side, two mounts of .50 caliber machine guns, and depth charges. We headed for Hawaii to be part of the Pacific Theater.

Once we arrived at Pearl Harbor, we saw the extent of the bombing the Japanese had inflicted. The place was pretty well blown up, and we weren't given any night liberty. In Honolulu we were to report back to the ship by 6:00 pm. When we came back from the invasion on our return trip, we were allowed out on the town at night. The problem was we were only allowed three drinks. Once we had our three drinks, we would go around and have three more drinks. We kind of got out of hand, and the MPs were called. They threw us into a motor oil truck, and our whites looked like they had been dragged through hog poo. I was never able to get them completely clean.

While in Hawaii, the ship was taking on supplies, and the number four gun turret was changed to magnetic minesweeping gear. We set out for Okinawa and did some minesweeping for a few months in the bay areas. We picked up quite a few mines. From the ship, we could see the big guns of the Japanese on the shore and observed our military and the Japanese during the invasion.

I grew very close to the men I served with. One of the gunner's mates could break down one of the five-inch guns blindfolded in less than three minutes. I got up to two and a half, but I wasn't blindfolded. The food wasn't gourmet, but we survived. On the way back, we had no kitchen, so we ate a lot of Spam and dehydrated eggs. A few of us figured out how to pass the time by cutting the ends off baked bread and adding a gallon of torpedo juice to get 190 proof alcohol out of it. We played a lot of pinochle, and a week before the invasion we were at general quarters at all times. I slept on a steel plate for a week, read, played cards, and wrote letters. Our gunner's mate was good at making things. On one occasion, he got some steel and made his mother a bracelet with her name engraved on it. Our Captain was an interesting man. On movie nights, we had to watch "Skipper" movies. He loved westerns, so all we watched were westerns. He didn't wear government issue side arms. The Captain wore pearl handled six-shooter pistols.

On April 1, 1945, general quarters were sounded at 6:00 am. I was a powder monkey in the gun turret. There were eight men inside this rotating five-inch cannon. I was sitting in a cage with my back against some rails and the tube of the gun in front of me. I loaded the powder case into the tube, which went into the gun turret. I was surrounded by cartridge cones and magazine powder.

At 7:00 am the invasion started. While we

were reloading, the lights went out and the door four feet behind me was blown off and hit my cage, throwing me onto the floor. We had been hit by a kamikaze, carrying a five hundred-pound bomb. The room was filled with flames. The kamikaze had struck just above the waterline on the ship, leaving a forty-by thirty-foot hole in the hull, and we were beached almost immediately. I scooted out onto the floor. Two men were already grabbing powder cases and cartridges, throwing them into the water to save further explosion. We went out into the chief's quarters, and the ladder to get down to the deck was gone. A bunk was found, and we used it to get out a porthole. None of my fellow turret-men were lost. Unfortunately, the men who were in the magazines near the explosion were killed, and the deck was blown up. We were instructed to move towards the fantail. We couldn't see anything because of the smoke. We all had a respect and trust for one another. We never got excited and we stayed calm. I don't know if we were too young to realize the danger, but we reacted just as we had been trained.

After the battle, fifty percent of the crew was transferred to other ships. The mess hall was gone, and there weren't enough undestroyed living quarters for the entire crew to stay on board. We spent thirty-nine days tied up for repairs. There was underwater welding day and night. We were stationed between two supply ships that were helping with supply, cleaning, and refitting the Forrester. Once repairs were finished, we simply reversed engines and headed back to Hawaii. As we were leaving, I could see P-38s and hear the machine guns. The whole ship would shake as they went by.

When I had a chance to talk with my family, I found out that at the instant my ship was hit, my sister was awakened. She remembers looking at the clock and wondering if I was okay.

LTJG Don Phillips
U.S.S. Achemar: WWII
Purple Heart

The U.S.S. Achemar was an attack/cargo ship. It had 30 landing craft and supplies in its hold. I was an ensign at 20 years old out of Norfolk, Virginia. I didn't know where we were going until we were underway. Our destination was Okinawa for the invasion of the Japanese islands. Since the battle was so close to the end of the war, it tends to be the forgotten battle. Some 250,000 Japanese civilians were killed in the attacks on Okinawa and 5,000 Americans lost their lives.

On April 1, 1945, 30 days after boarding the ship, we had reached Okinawa. On the day of the invasion, the bridge of a nearby ship was hit by a kamikaze. Most were either killed or wounded by the blast. About 150 ships were hit by kamikazes on the day of the invasion just as we were hitting the beaches. There was little resistance to the landing forces because the Japanese had dug into the hills and were waiting for the advancing troops.

During the night, over 500 kamikaze moonlight raids pelted our ships. I was hit with shrapnel when our ship was hit. The plane smashed into the deck, and I was 500 feet away. The shrapnel penetrated the one-inch steel plating and ripped the surrounding structures apart. One of the officers said he would give his left arm to get out of this, and his left arm was blown off. What saved our ship was the boom wires. These cables ripped the planes apart before they made impact. We had a young sailor put a rosary in the bridge and say a blessing over our bridge. Our bridge was never hit.

It was the largest armada ever assembled in history. At night we made smoke with smoke machines to hide the fleet from kamikazes. All guns were manned at quarters at all times. We had a group of Marines on our ship who were night fighters. They were the first unit on the beaches to soften up the beachhead and check for resistance.

89

We could tell when the planes were coming because of radar.

In the end, I was glad to be going home. We had shot down many planes that were aimed straight for us. Men had itchy trigger fingers and were shooting at everything that flew. A U.S. pilot was shot down taking off from a carrier because everyone was on edge from the kamikaze raids. The convoy constantly zigzagged, and we fixed the ship when we got back to Hawaii. When we were under attack, one young kid was hammering wooden plugs into the holes of our hull to prevent us from sinking. Airplanes were buzzing by as he was welding.

When I got back, I was able to put myself through college and buy a home on the GI Bill. Farm kids could go to night classes on the GI Bill and get the farm going during the day. I may not agree with everything we do as a country, but I am proud to be an American. This country helped save lives, and it brought us home safe and sound.

PFC Elmer Salini
United States Army Medical Corp
Hawaiian Islands

Elmer Salini: Honolulu, Hawaii—1944

I was drafted in November, 1942, and was
sent to the Presidio in Monterey. I wasn't sad, I

wasn't thrilled – it was a job for us to do. I didn't have a real good job in Stockton. I was put in the Medical Corps, so I didn't have to go to boot camp. For some reason, I was kept out of harm's way during the war. It seemed that because of the decisions I made, along with just plain luck, I was the luckiest guy to go through World War II.

When we took off from Monterey, there were three separate groups that went out on that day. As I marched in a covered space with one group along one side of me and another group along the other side, I had no idea where we were being sent. We had tags on our duffle bags that revealed our destinations. I hadn't looked at my tag yet, but I asked a guy on my left what his tag said and he said, "McClellan Field, Sacramento." I asked the guy on the other side, and he said, "Stockton Field," so I figured I better look at my tag. It said "Presidio of San Francisco," and I said, "Good! The safest place in the world!"

So we got on the train from Monterey, and it took us to the Presidio of San Francisco. We were put in with an MP barracks group to bunk with for the night. The next day when they looked at my stature – I was 5'7" or 5'8"—they told me that I was too small to be an MP, so they sent me over to the Medical Corps.

Before I was shipped overseas to Hawaii in the spring of '43, I was working with civilians in the kitchen in Spokane, WA. I was told that I was going to get shipped out overseas in a few weeks, so I told these civilians that I was shipping out and going into combat. They gave me a party, but a week before I was supposed to leave, the sergeant came up to me and said, "Well we looked on your record and you are due a furlough, so we can take you off the overseas list." But I said to the sergeant, "Those civilians threw me a party because they thought that I was leaving and now I'm staying. What am I gonna do?" I told him to put me back on the overseas list, which turned out to be the best decision I ever made because they shipped me to the Hawaiian Islands.

When the ship reached Hawaii, they told me to get off, and I spent two years in Hawaii. It was lucky that soldiers were needed in Hawaii. I saw many wounded soldiers during my two years, but the worst were the mental patients. There was one guy, a Marine, who had fought in the battle of Iwo Jima. He was blindfolded when he came in. I asked another Marine what had happened to him and he said, "Shrapnel went through him and just cut his eyes to pieces."

It's awful what happened to these guys—legs amputated, eyes gone—it was awful. I'll never forget the tormented young men I met while working in the psychiatric ward. Not many people seem to be aware of what war can do to a soldier's mind, but I'll never forget.

In 1945, during the last six months of the war, I was teed-off because everyone else was making corporal and sergeant and I was still a PFC. I told them that I was ashamed to go home now because I was still a PFC. They said, "We didn't know you wanted a promotion." So, I said, "Yeah, I want a promotion. I don't want to boss anybody, but that extra money comes in handy!"

Before the U.S. dropped the bomb on Japan, I was interviewed by an officer who was interviewing a bunch of other guys, and he asked me if I thought I could walk or march twenty-five miles. I said, "I've never tried it, sir. Maybe I can, maybe I can't." It wasn't until later that I realized that I had been slated to go over for the invasion of Japan. I was against the bomb when it was dropped—even though it saved my life. Once again I was diverted from combat.

When the war was over and it was time to go back to the mainland, we were set up in tent cities where we waited for transport. We were there about three or four days before they started putting us on airplanes. Then they ran out of room on the planes, so they started putting us on ships. They announced that everybody who wanted to go back home by ship should go sign up, so everybody went and signed up because they wanted to take advantage of their chance to get back home. I had a different plan. I told a guy who I didn't really know, but who was in my tent, that if there was a plane leaving within the next two or three days, we would beat the guys on the ship home. I don't know what had gotten into me that day, but I just felt that we should wait for a plane.

The next morning all the guys were ready and packed to leave on the ship, and this guy and I were the only two guys left in the tent city. I said to myself, "For me, I don't care, but I talked this other guy into staying, and now I feel bad!" At about five o'clock that evening, I told the guy that I was going over to the USO and if someone came and said there was a plane leaving, to come and get me. At around 5:30, here came the guy. He ran all the way to tell me that a plane was leaving and they had room for two more guys. We got on the plane, which was filled with officers but had space for just two more men. So, we beat the guys on the ship home. Just another good decision I made during WWII!

In 1945 I was working on the night shift. Night duty was from 6:00 p.m. until 6:00 a.m. The Signal Corps came around one day and installed a telephone by a bed in the ward, and I said to the nurse, "What's going on – putting a phone in the ward?" She said, "We are getting General Robert C. Richardson, Jr. in tomorrow." He was coming in for minor surgery.

The next day, when I got on duty at six o'clock, I didn't fool around with the general. He was the commander of the Middle Pacific Area during WWII, and like the President of the United States to us GIs. At about nine o'clock, the nurse came over to me and said, "I forgot a pitcher of water on the bed stand in the general's room." The general was not supposed to have any food to eat or water to drink. So the nurse said, "Take off your shoes and go get the pitcher of water."

I was only a PFC, so I had to do what she said. The front door of the ward was open to let in the breeze because it was always very hot and humid in Hawaii. So I was sneaking into where the general was, going slowly, slowly, and all of a sudden, a gust of wind slammed the front door shut just as I was about the grab the water pitcher! The general opened up his eyes and mumbled something to me and I said, "I'm sorry, general, but I got to get this water out of here." "Okay," he said.

So that's how I accidentally woke up the general, which turned out to be the closest I ever came to real danger. I was scared out of my wits. There weren't too many PFC's who had contact with a general.

Chief Signalman Delton E. Walling
U.S. Navy: WWII
Seven Service Awards

While I was in high school, all I could think about when I graduated was joining the Navy. So I graduated on June 21st, and on June 22nd, another young fellow and I hitchhiked from where we lived in Michigan to Detroit, 200 miles away. We were buddies all through school so we went together.

When we got down there, the Navy took him but they didn't take me. When we got up there for the physical and were standing there, bare butt and all, the doctor said, "Move your hands." I moved them fast, but I didn't move them fast enough because one of my fingers was stiff and I couldn't flex it that well. Well, the doctor said, "You're going to be 4-F because you have a finger that's stiff." I said, "Hey, wait a minute. What do I have to do? I want to go in the Navy with my buddy." The doctor said, "Well you have to cut it off." I said, "Alright, make out a form so I can do this." I left and started hitching back home.

I got to Lansing, Michigan, where a guy let me out. I started walking around when I noticed a sign that said, "Surgeon." I showed the surgeon the form and told him what I wanted. He said, "You're crazy, I won't do it." I said, "I'll find somebody else if you don't." He agreed to do it. I said, "Look, I only have twenty dollars and I still have 100 miles to hitchhike. Could you leave me enough to get a hamburger?" He said, "Sure; I'll cut it off for seventeen dollars."

I stuck my hand in my shirt and hitched the rest of the way home. My parents weren't too happy. On July 9, 1940, I reported to Great Lakes Naval Station.

First of all, I want it understood that I am no hero because, look, if there are heroes, they were all heroes. You have to understand the war was won with kids from 17 to 25 years old. No matter where you put them that's where they were. That's the kids who died out there in the Pacific. I just happened to be in the wrong spot in Pearl Harbor, and all I did was do my job just like any body else.

Editor's Note: Chief Petty Officer Walling was a Chief Signalman with Admiral Richardson's staff, then Admiral Kimmel's staff, and finally Admiral Nimitz's staff.

Staff Sgt. Merle E. Warner
8th Air Force- 401 BG -615 Bomb Squadron
European Theater: WWII
P.O.W. Medal, Air Medal, Purple Heart

Merle Warner: Deenethorpe, England—1945

On May 15, 1944, our crew was taken to the
air base at Deenethorpe, England. This was base

number 128 and home of the 401st Bombardment Group. This was part of the Eighth Air Force that was under the command of General James Doolittle.

For the twelve days prior to the first mission, we flew some practice flights, attended a refresher course in gunnery school, and were issued our equipment and also a military .45 pistol. Most of my free time on the base was spent writing letters home; reading, watching planes returning from their missions, and watching my buddies play poker. At the base, there was a box for monetary donations to buy cigarettes for P.O.W.s. Even though I did not smoke, it never occurred to me that I would ever become a P.O.W.

We were never informed of our missions in advance. Around 4 a.m. was our wake up call, then breakfast, and then our briefing. We were given flight instructions, target locations, maps, a compass, and pills to take if needed to stay awake. A truck took each crew to their assigned plane where we readied the plane for takeoff. After we reached our flying altitude, we flew in tight formation to prevent enemy fighter planes from getting through. Occasionally, we were hit with flak. Once, I counted one hundred and eighty-five bullet holes just in the right wing. My crew flew missions over Germany and France. On D-Day, we protected the beachheads in Bayeux, France.

My last mission on July 7 near Leipzig, Germany, was when we lost one engine to an oil leak and another to enemy fire. The plane caught on fire and began a nosedive. We had had no training in "bailing out." The radio operator tried to open the door, but it was stuck. I pulled out the door pins and kicked the door open. I then pushed the shocked radio operator out and threw myself behind him. I quickly counted ten and pulled the ripcord. I landed in a pasture, buried my chute, and began crawling away from the site. I was soon captured and taken to a small building. There, many of my flight crew members were already being held.

The next day the Germans took us by train to Frankfurt, where we were interrogated. I spent ten days in solitary confinement because the interrogating officer didn't like my answer to his question. In a five-foot by eight-foot cell with only a cup of soup and a slice of bread to eat daily, I spent most of my time talking to God and wondering how long the war would last.

Then I was taken to Stalag Luft IV near the Baltic Sea. Here, we were photographed, strip searched, and further incarcerated. I was not physically mistreated; however, one day I observed other prisoners being transferred to our camp. The guards bayonets poked into their behinds and guard dogs bit the prisoners' legs.

When I first arrived, the weather was in the seventies, but soon the weather grew cooler, and when it rained we were cold. The building had no insulation and only a small stove to burn a rationed bar of coal. Some months it snowed, and that left us to depend on each other's body warmth. At night, we only had a single bulb to play cards by. It was often pitch dark late at night as the generators were turned off. This meant feeling our way along the walls and counting the doors when we needed to use the latrine. Many of us often fought a battle with diarrhea.

Our food was served at midday, usually a boiled potato and a slice of bread. Thank God for the Red Cross packages we received about every two months. Items included were a can of Spam, vegetables, a box of sugar, a chocolate bar, margarine, prunes, jam, powdered milk, two cans of fish, instant coffee, cigarettes, cheese, soap, and crackers.

On February 6, 1945, the Russian Army was fast approaching our camp from the east. The Germans feared being captured by the Russians, as they were known to be ruthless and would kill anyone who stood in their way. Our captors told us we would be moved to another camp and the march would take a week. Little did we know we would be marching for eighty days.

My clothes were infested with lice and my socks were rotted to my flesh. The pain of walking was unbearable as my feet were sore and blistered. I estimated I had lost fifty pounds during my captivity. There were times I thought I would never see freedom again.

On April 26, 1945, we were liberated by the 104th Division of the U.S. Army. C-47's flew us to Rheims, France, where I had my first shower since the march had begun. We were loaded aboard ship, which docked at Virginia. From there, the train took us to Camp Beale in Marysville, California.

It is difficult to put into words the emotions I felt as I saw my wife, Ella, waiting for me. As we hugged each other, it almost seemed like time had stood still and that I hadn't been away. Until then, I hadn't let myself think about home too much. I just lived from day to day and concentrated on staying alive so I would be able to go home when the war ended.

Lt. Frederick Weybret
Navy LST 728: WWII
American Campaign, Asiatic Pacific with Star

Fred Weybret: January 20, 1944

There was just no question in my mind that when I was in Diesel School, most of the training was oriented towards the amphibious boats. LST was where I eventually ended up. Most of our training was directed to the equipment aboard those vessels. When I finished at Raleigh, I was sent for LST training at Camp Redford, VA, as an engineering officer.

LST 728 was my boat. It had 4000 tons of displacement—328 feet long, 50 feet wide—and could probably hold three to four hundred men. But we also hauled their machinery. Tanks. Supplies.

At Okinawa, we went in on D-Day. Our basic cargo was troops and what they called Amtracks—amphibious tractors. So we launched these several hundred yards, half a mile off the beach. We didn't go in to the beach until D plus 8. We waited those eight days for the balance of our cargo, and the balance of our cargo was 400 tons of mortar ammunition. The whole cap deck had been first laid down with crates of mortar ammunition, and then timbers were laid across them and the Amtracks rode on top of that when we went in. We used to wonder down in the engine room right under that, "If they got us would we be blown up or down?" Fortunately, we never found out. I don't think we'd have known the difference. There was about an inch of steel plate between where I spent General Quarters in the engine room and those mortars.

I remember the night we unloaded that ammunition. It was kind of interesting. They sent a work party of Seabees down with some small trucks. They could drive up on the ship, load the ammunition up, and take it off. And they'd just started doing that when the Kamikazes really came in. Those men just took off—moved. They just disappeared, but they left the trucks. So the First Lieutenant and I talked with the Captain and said, "Here are these trucks and tons of ammunition that we don't really want."

We put together a work party, and that night we unloaded our own ship. We'd never had a group volunteer for a work party like that. Everybody on the ship turned out. We used the Seabees' trucks, and by next morning we backed off the beach. We were done. We left their trucks. We just could hardly wait to get rid of that stuff.

Cpl. Frank Wright
4th Marine Raider, 21st Marines: WWII
Two Purple Hearts & Presidential Unit Citations

Frank Wright: Tongue Point Naval Air Station—1942

February 19, 1945, was the date when Iwo Jima was hit. There were so many days of bombing, so many days of ships sending their salvos in on the island, that we just figured that nothing could be alive on the island. My company went in on the June 21, and our forces had just gotten off the beach. The first people to hit the beach were just slaughtered in this black volcanic sand. There were bodies, heads, and legs. These were our men lying there—our men. All these bombs and all these salvos had done hardly any damage because all the Japanese went underground. The island was just honeycombed with tunnels.

They hadn't secured the island, and the first flag raising was right at the top of Mt. Suribachi. I didn't see the first raising because the flag was small. They said, "We want something that everyone can see." So they sent a man down the mountain, and he got onto a boat, went over to one of the ships, and got a large flag. He came back, fought his way back up. That's when Joe Rosenthal set the guys up. He said, "You, you, and you—push that flag up." I saw that one. I got chills . . . chills all over my body. When you see the flag, you want to cry and your nose is tingly and your eyes get wet. We saw the flag, and then everybody yelled and hollered, and we took off.

I got hit in the head with a rifle slug. It hit my helmet and knocked me out, and I fell down into a hole. My squad thought I was dead. The second group that came up behind me checked, and I was okay. I asked where my company was, and they said they'd gone, on so I went after them. I went through an area my group had already passed, and a Jap popped out of this fighter hole and was aiming at the guys behind me. I turned around just in time and saw him, and I just pulled my trigger three or four times. There was another Jap, his partner, inside the spider hole (a hole about four feet around that goes straight down) and then I shot him.

On March 3, we were gong up over a little rise just before the beach. We were in a pincher movement. My scout was a guy by the name of Navaho. My BAR was Speed McCoy. Navaho went over the hill and stood up there. Speed came up, stood up there, and looked around. I went up, and a Japanese machine gun opened up on me and sprayed me across my chest, my lungs, my clavicle, and my left arm. I went down. Speed McCoy pulled me into a shell hole, and he stayed with me for a while. But when he went back up over the ridge, somebody threw a hand grenade at him. He must've gotten two to three hundred fragments in the back of his body from his heel clear up to his neck—just potholed, and blood was just popping up all over his body, so he just turned right around and came back into the hole with me.

I was going through shock. A corpsman came up and gave me plasma—he had it right with him. You'll never find a Marine that didn't love the corpsmen; they are just lifesavers, period. He held the little plastic bag, and a grenade came in and blew up right behind the corpsman and took his two fingers off just like that. He didn't drop the bag. He didn't drop the bag. He just held it up like that.

After the bag got empty, he put it down and put bandages on his hand.

We waited for the stretcher carriers to come in, and they weren't coming in, so McCoy and I walked about two miles back to the beach. I don't know how long it took us. They were bandaging my arm, and I said, "I feel really wet back here." When I rubbed my hand on my chest, I put my fingers right into my chest. Until then I didn't know I had been shot there. At that time I was smoking, and so I had to have a cigarette. I would inhale the smoke and the smoke would come out of the hole.

I have two Purple Hearts, one for my stomach and one for my chest wound. A little Navy Wave massaged my hands, my arm, and my shoulder, and pretty soon I had full use of it—not as strong as it was—but full use.

KOREAN WAR

Col. Wilson Heefner
Osaka Army Hospital: Korea
Legion of Merit

I enlisted in the U.S. Army in July, 1949, one month after graduating from high school in Waynesboro, Pennsylvania. I had originally planned to attend college and medical school, but financial problems precluded that, so I elected to join the service to receive training in the medical field. I underwent basic training at Fort Dix, New Jersey, and found it to be an eye-opening experience, learning close order drill, military discipline, and how to live in a field environment, and firing the various weapons common to the infantry.

In November, I was transferred to Fort Sam Houston, Texas, where I completed sixteen weeks of schooling to qualify me as a medical laboratory technician. In May, 1950, I shipped out from San Francisco for Japan, where I was assigned to Osaka

Army Hospital. Less than a month after my arrival in Osaka, the Korean War began. Although many officers and enlisted men from my hospital were sent to Korea to "flesh out" the medical assets of the deploying combat forces, I remained in Osaka, where I served as a medical laboratory technician for the next fifteen months.

The North Korean attack came as a complete surprise to virtually everyone, but most of us felt the war would be short-lived. However, the American forces were under strength, poorly trained, and poorly conditioned, and were further handicapped by poorly maintained and worn-out vehicles, armor, and weapons. Many categories of ammunition, particularly for the artillery, were also quite low. As a result, the American forces found themselves forced to withdraw continually toward Pusan, suffering very heavy casualties. Many of those casualties were evacuated to our hospital, and because we were so understaffed, we found ourselves working very long hours for many months. The landing at Inchon in September, 1950, temporarily reversed the situation, allowing our forces to advance into North Korea, but the intervention of the Chinese Communist Forces in October and November caused American casualties to soar and forced our withdrawal from North Korea. Many of the casualties suffered from frostbite, and the great majority of those casualties became patients at Osaka.

Among my most vivid memories was seeing the large number of acquaintances from my basic training days and my time in medical laboratory school who were wounded in Korea and who were evacuated to our hospital. As I talked with them about their experiences in combat, I thanked God that I had been spared such experiences. Among my pleasant memories are the visits by numerous celebrities to raise the morale of the casualties: Al Jolson, Bob Hope, Marilyn Maxwell, Joe DiMaggio, and Lefty O'Doul.

My service at Osaka Army Hospital was very

rewarding, and greatly influenced my subsequent medical career. I also developed a deep affection for the Japanese people, and in 1976 returned to Japan with my wife, son, and daughter, where we visited the hospital where I had served, now a Japanese hospital.

I left Osaka in September, 1951, and spent the rest of my enlistment stateside. Following my discharge in December, 1952, with the rank of corporal, I attended college and medical school, utilizing the G.I. Bill. My medical specialties were pathology and nuclear medicine. I continued my military career in the Army National Guard and the U.S. Army Reserve, retiring in 1990 as a Colonel after forty-one years of service.

Cpt. Walter E. Jeghers
65th Regiment, 3rd Infantry Division: Korea
Combat Infantry Badge, National Defense

About six weeks before I graduated from an R.O.T.C. program in college, I got orders to report for active duty. After basic training at Fort Hood in Texas, I was on my way to Korea. When I got to Korea, I was made a platoon leader. I was put in charge of 40 men. These were my men, all 40 of them. That means I lived with them, ate with them, slept with them; I was with them twenty-four hours a day. I got to know them. I got to know them pretty well. In this platoon, thankfully, I had a platoon sergeant whom I relied on a lot. I was young and inexperienced. He was older, a WW II vet with combat experience.

The worst part of the war was over by the time I got over there. It was pretty much a stalemate along the 38th parallel. The Korean War had turned into what was called "the hill wars." We fought over these hills—like Pork Chop Hill, Old Baldie, Heart Break Ridge and the Iron Triangle—because whoever had the high ground had the advantage. These were all strategic areas of fighting. We would take a hill from the enemy, and they would take it right back from us. That was mainly what the last part of the war was like.

We would always send out patrols, recon, and combat to see what they were doing. Mostly there were the artillery duels between their side and ours. I remember there was a lot of artillery in both directions. This was hard on the nerves and ears. Along the 38th parallel, we were dug in pretty well. We had built bunkers with peepholes in them, so we could shoot out. These bunkers were connected together with trenches. We could go anywhere without exposing ourselves, which was a good thing because they were always throwing artillery at us. Thankfully, we didn't lose too many men to their artillery.

Most of our line was in the mountain areas.

The elevation was around five to six thousand feet. You know, whenever we did assault a hill, our artillery and Air Force made the job a little easier.

I have to say the weather was one of the most miserable things about the whole experience. In the winter it was very cold, and in the summer it was hot, humid, and raining, it seemed like, all the time.

Out of my company, we lost about 12 men out of 200. I was fortunate that I missed the worst part of the war. I am thankful for that.

Lt. Colonel Cecil Kramer
Airman 2nd Class
548th Photo Recon: Korea
Good Conduct Medal

I love airplanes and have always wanted to fly. I received a draft notice in the mail, but I didn't want to report to the Army, so I joined the Air Force in 1954. My basic training took place at Parks Air Force Base in the Livermore area. Afterwards, I was transferred to Cheyenne, Wyoming, where I was asked to be a demolitions expert. I turned down the offer because I wanted to fly. I worked for the Inspector General and was assigned to the 548th Photo Recon in Japan. I was part of an airbase defense team for two years.

My first days of service were quite diverse. One of our guys went AWOL because he couldn't take the discipline. Some of the guys had never had discipline before. About four weeks later, our sergeant found him and brought him back. The sergeant didn't list him as AWOL. He went out on a limb. He didn't want to treat him harshly but wanted him to realize that they were being trained for combat. The sergeant never judged him for why he went; instead the sergeant turned him around rather than turn him over to the MPs. I will always remember our drill instructor. He treated us fairly, and I would follow him anywhere.

While I was in training, I got sick and didn't know it. In full field gear, running uphill, I thought I had a sprained ankle. After an hour, I couldn't walk and went on sick leave. When we were shipping out, after I got out of the hospital, I was running with full field gear and fell, breaking my knee and wrist. I called the base and walked up a flight of stairs to the hospital. I spent the next few months in the hospital, paralyzed with rheumatic fever, and lost my chance of ever becoming a pilot.

During Korea, I was stationed in Japan. Serving in the Air Force, I was able to get top secret clearance and knew a lot about what was going on in my area. I was sent to Korea once with a detachment of soldiers on loan to a group of soldiers who were short-handed. The winter was cold, and we lived in tents. We were never able to get warm and operated off a dirt runway. I worked in the photo lab as an assistant and wrote death letters home to the families of men who had died in battle. It was hard to write about someone you knew and watch their belongings get sent back home. I did my best to make the letters personal and heartfelt. Korea was a cold, dirty war, but I loved Japan.

The people of Japan were really nice, and I never hung around the bars, so I was able to make friends with some Japanese businessmen. I was invited to weddings and parties and spent many days as a guest in families' homes. They treated me very well, even though most didn't have much to spare. I brought them nylons and raviolis, and they thought I was giving them the world. One of the men I knew gave me a 1950 Mercury to drive, and I loved riding around Japan in my off-duty hours.

Even with the Japanese military, I was able to make friends. One day I switched uniforms with a soldier, and we took a picture together.

I would frequent the Club Zanzibar and eat a steak dinner for $.70. The Air Force had excellent food, and we were never out of supplies. In Japan we even had a gambling place with slot machines in a pool hall where service men could unwind. On the weekends, I would go sightseeing with my Japanese friends. I went to the Emperor's palace, which was uncommon for the average person to even be allowed to do. I was impressed with the beauty of the statues of Buddha and the mountains that were simply built with nature.

On May Day, the communists had a big march and attacked our base. We had Japanese defense forces, which were under our guidance. The communists tore down the fences and ran vehicles into the base. They wanted to destroy our planes. The Japanese defense force stopped the communists, and no shots were fired. The riot only lasted a couple of hours.

There was no pressure or stress for me after my service. I only wish I had extended my service, and I often think of the friends I left behind.

Lt. William E. Latham, M.D.

U.S. Navy

3rd Battalion, 1st Marines: Korea

When the Navy re-activated me in 1950, I was immediately loaned out to the Army. I was assigned to Camp Cook, which was not ready, so I was sent to Lompoc military prison where I helped out the doctors during the day and was locked down for security at night. Thankfully, the Navy took me back.

Six months later, a Navy corpsman came running up and told me that I was loaned out to the Marines. I was to report to Camp Pendleton for training to eventually go to Korea. In basic, I was given a M-1 rifle and taught how to use it. When I landed in Korea, a sergeant came up to me and told me, "Sir, you're not going to need that M-1. You're going to need this," and he gave me a .45. He then told me that "if anything happens, it will be close combat." That made me a little nervous.

When I got to Korea, I kept drawing the short straw. In Korea it was set up like this: first there was Division, then there was Regiment, then M.A.S.H., then Battalion, and finally the forward aid station. I started out at Regiment, and by the luck of the short straw moved up to Battalion, which is where the fighting was going on. I could hear the artillery shells going over my head. I drew the short straw again and moved up to forward aid station, the one in the trenches where the artillery shells I once heard over my head were now landing.

This was my first day in Korea. It was winter, cold, the Manchurian winds, minus temperatures; everything was frozen. In the morning, there were about five or six poor North Koreans frozen on the barbed wire about 100 feet from where I was. They had infiltrated during the night. I knew what was going on, but the Marines—I always felt that this was the greatest thing—the Marines always took care of their medical people. I am glad I was with them. They knew what was important for their survival. They always kept us doctors informed about what to expect, whether we needed to put our packs on and go forward or back.

This was quite an experience for someone who was not a war person. I was over in Korea for about a year. I spent six weeks on the front line. Then we went into reserves and then back to the front line. I was eventually sent to Pyongyang, on the west coast, then on to Inchon where it became my duty to go out to the hospital ship and help out with the wounded.

William Edward Pfeifle
Aviation Structural Mechanic 3rd Class:
Korean War
Good Conduct, Navy Occupation (European Clasp)

William Pfeifle: Palermo, Sicily—Summer 1952

I wasn't drafted; I joined up myself. I took my induction in Bismarck, North Dakota. I had always wanted to go into the Navy. I was born in

1932 and had grown up during World War II. I remember at that time thinking, "How long is this thing going to last?" At that time they were drafting people at 17 ½ years old, and many were lying about their ages just so they could get in even younger. So as soon as I got an opportunity to enlist, I did. A lot of my friends waited until the last minute, and the Army got them. They were stuck. I received letters from some guys complaining about what a raw deal they had, but I didn't have much sympathy because they had had plenty of time to join up before the draft.

A friend of mine and I both went into the Navy. We got on the train in Aberdeen, South Dakota. We took the Northshore Railroad that goes into Chicago by way of a loop that loops downtown near the elevated system. As a rule, they ran on time in the evening, but we got in there and apparently we had just missed the train and had to wait 45 minutes to an hour for the next train. When we got down to the Great Lakes Naval Training

Station, which was south of Milwaukee, I'll never forget. We walked up to the guard's shack, and the guy asked who we were. After we gave him our envelopes, he looked at our names and said, "You're late." That was the start of the Navy for us.

When people ask me if I would do it over again, I jokingly reply, "Well, if you could spend your summers in the Mediterranean and your winters in Florida, what else would you want? I mean that's where I was sent." I had two "Med" cruises. I was on the Carrier U.S.S. Oriskany, in `51 and on the Carrier U.S.S. Coral Sea, in `52. Then I went to Korea in `53 on the Carrier, U.S.S. Lake Champlain.

We had a couple of shakedown cruises where we qualified pilots off the coasts of Cuba and Haiti. We would be out there maybe a week, although we'd be on the ship a little longer. We frequently went on night operations during which the pilots would have to make at least 10 to 15 landings each night while everything was blacked out. I would volunteer for that duty because it kept me off the base. In those days, we had a Signal Officer standing on a little platform in the back, and he used these wands to bring in the pilots. The planes were all propeller-driven aircraft, except for some of the jets we had. We had two squadrons of jets. The rest were Corsairs and Douglas Sky Raiders. We could tell the difference in the aircraft's engine sounds, so we knew when ours were coming in. I'd watch the Signal Officer, and if he was doing a regular landing, that was fine.

My job was to check the flaps and make sure the landing gear was locked and secured. By the time we did that, one guy working from each side of the plane, the Launch Officer would already have given the pilot the line depth which prompted the pilot to turn up his engines so he was ready to go. At that point we would be caught in the prop wash. So I just went to my side of the ship and waited for the next plane to come. We had red wands because you could not have any bright lights on the carrier at night.

Sometimes we had to work 72 hours straight because we had so many aircraft that needed to go out. We were constantly working. I was a metalsmith, so when someone got shot we would patch up the holes. Sometimes we did hydraulic work and things like that. It was a never-ending process; it just kept going.

There is one piece of memorabilia that I carry from the war. It is my "shellback" card. There was a ritual that was performed on a ship whenever it crossed the equator. Every service member on the ship, regardless of rank, was put through a ceremony if it was their first time crossing the equator. They were made to crawl through garbage chutes and other mildly torturous pranks. Once a man was put through the ritual and got his "shellback" card, he never had to go through it again. It was like a rite of passage for Navy men.

VIETNAM WAR

MSCM John Britto
U.S.S. Jennings County: Vietnam
Navy Commendation Medal

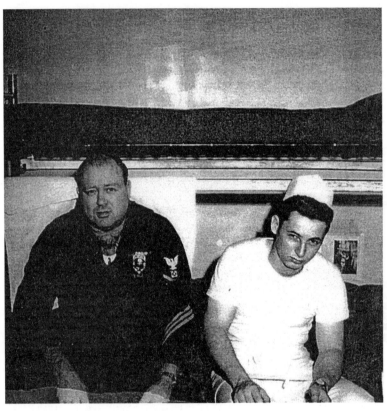

John Britto (right) and Bo' sun Page: Adak, Alaska—1963

As the ship I was on came into the river patrol boat base, there was a message from the commanding officer that said, "As soon as your ship drops anchor, I want to see your ship's cook." That was me, and I thought to myself, "Most unusual." The boat that they sent out was a rag-tag, rough looking group. They'd been there awhile, seasoned veterans. So I climbed down the ladder, got into this boat, and went away.

When the boat landed, they said, "The Skipper's up there." So I climbed up the hill to this hut and I introduced myself. He said, "You're responsible for feeding my men. They're not eating very well and I want you to fix it. Today!" I said, "Yes sir. Where's the galley? Where do you cook here?" He called some guys, and we walked down this dirt path to a mud hut.

Inside, there were two Sears & Roebuck refrigerators that had seen better days; much better days. And then they had shelves with food in various stages of wellness—it was really not good stuff—and boxes and cans and so forth. I asked, "Well, who's in charge here?" because at that time there were sixty-five men at this outpost. They pointed to this kid who was like nineteen years old, and he was scared to death. He said, "I've just come here, and the guy that was here before me didn't do very well and he didn't train me. And the guys on the ship who are supposed to help me, they haven't helped, and I don't know what to do." He was almost in tears.

At that time, we cooked with a Mark-1937 field range. It took gasoline, and we put it under pressure. They were very big, very dangerous, and they blew up with regularity. There was no way to cook, except that. We had also to heat our own water to wash dishes. We always had to do that and keep water hot for our utensils and so forth, so we were always moving pots of water. Based on our skill level, our ingenuity, and our use of time, it was very difficult to make three meals a day for sixty-five people, especially if one was nineteen and did not have any experience.

So I called back on the radio and told what the situation was, and said, "Send the following items." And they did, pretty quick. That night I stayed and I worked with the kid and made this meal. And it was the best meal they'd had in months. That commanding officer and I became the best of buddies for the year that we were there.

Chief Warrant Officer Alan Fink
195th Assault Helicopter Company: Vietnam
Distinguished Flying Cross

Alan Fink: III Corps Area—early 1968

We were based at Quan Loi, which was an airstrip in the middle of a Michelin rubber plantation. It was in the middle of the monsoon season, and we were actually living in the rubber plantation itself in tents, and the officer's club was set up as a tent. One day we had what they call a "maintenance stand-down," and our Commander told us that we could all go to the officers' club and have a good time. It was raining absolute cats and dogs, and we went into the club and had a few toots, starting at about 5 o' clock in the evening.

About 10 o'clock, the First Sergeant threw open the tent flap into the rain and wind and said, "Hey, I need the two most sober pilots in here." Well, it just so turned out that I was one of the most sober pilots in there. The fellow that was with me was an American Indian who did not drink at all, so he was obviously sober. The only problem with him was that he was a gunship pilot and the First Sergeant needed a lift helicopter or a "slick" to fly this mission. I looked over at him and said, "Well, I guess that's us. What's the story? What do you need?"

The First Sergeant said we had a walk-out

patrol that had just been ambushed right outside the perimeter of the base. They had some seriously wounded, needed a Med Evac right away, and they were still under fire. So we ran over to the other tent, grabbed our helmets and weapons, and found a helicopter. He briefed us on where they were, which turned out to be no more than probably a couple of thousand feet from where we were parked, but they were outside the wire and they were pinned down. The problem was that where we had to land was steep, sloping terrain that had been bombed, mortared, chopped up, bulldozed, and everything else, so there was no real spot to actually land the aircraft. I placed the "uphill" skid against the slope and just held the helicopter at a hover while the four guys on the ground loaded their three wounded comrades.

After they loaded the three wounded, I basically picked the helicopter up, rolled it to the left, and landed straight in to the Med Evac Pad next to the main airstrip. When the doctor and the nurses walked up to the helicopter, the doctor got into the cargo compartment with the wounded. With his flashlight, he could see they were severely wounded. One had a wound to the back of his head. Another one had been hit in the back, probably with a grenade or rocket, and this had basically removed his back from his waistline to the back of his skull, but he was still alive. I couldn't see the third guy because he was almost directly behind my seat, but I believe he had a stomach wound.

Then the doctor reached up on the overhead and turned on the white light, which shocked and surprised all of us. We almost never used lights in Viet Nam, as they tended to attract bullets. He tapped me on the shoulder, and I swung my microphone around on my helmet so he could speak to me. What he said was, "I can't do anything for them. They have to go to 124th Evac hospital at Long Binh," which was about a thirty-five minute flight. The gunship pilot rarely flew in the clouds for what we called instrument flying. We all had basically minimal instrument flying experience, so there weren't very many of us who had the confidence or any real skill doing it. It's very, very hazardous anyway if we don't know what we're doing.

I explained to the doctor that we couldn't fly them there tonight in that weather because there was a monsoon cold front moving through the area: severe turbulence, lightening, thunder, high winds and so forth. He replied, "Well, if you don't, they're going to die right here on the pad." I looked at the gunship pilot, and he looked at me and said, "What do you think?" I said, "Well, we have no choice; we're going to go."

The medical people cleared the area and we got up the rotor speed. I called the Air Traffic Control Center in Saigon, gave them my flight plan, and told them to also shut down all the artillery because it was a medical emergency and we didn't have time to fool around with taking a chance of being shot down by our own guys. And they did.

We did not have any weather radar in the helicopter, so the center controllers had to guide us through the storm. The doors of the aircraft were pinned in the open position, and the casualties were lying on the metal floor. As we proceeded to Long Binh, the rain was coming in the helicopter because of the air flow, and the crew, the casualties, everything was soaking wet. There was water running everywhere.

As we were about ten minutes from landing at Long Binh, I felt a tap on my shoulder and I turned my head to the right. On the center console of the helicopter, where the radio and some of the system switches were, the casualty that had no back was sitting there, tapping me on the shoulder, trying to get my attention. I swung my microphone around and keyed the microphone switch, and he said, "Boy, sir, this shit really looks dangerous. I'm sure glad I don't have to do this." And I could literally see his spine from the base of his skull to his belt line. The muscle, tissue, everything was gone.

We got all three casualties down there, and

when we got ready to land at 124 Evac, we had broken through the storm. The weather at the hospital pad was actually very good. But unfortunately all three of them ended up dying anyway.

PFC Jay Lawson

33rd Ordnance Company: Vietnam

Jay Lawson: Vietnam—1966

They called us "ammo humpers." We'd just physically swing boxes, load stuff, and pack things. It was very hard, strenuous work. We were working one night, and twenty-five hundred pounds of ammunition stacked on a couple of pallets got knocked over. I tried getting out of the way. There was a little bank right beside it, surrounded by little berms, and I tried to back pedal up. If I hadn't, it would have landed right on top of me and crushed me. I didn't make it all the way up the bank, so the pallets landed right in the middle of both legs.

I don't know why, but it only broke one leg. I yelled, yelled, yelled, and the men got the ammunition off and I tried to stand up, but it was like standing on a noodle. It was like I was floating; I wasn't even aware of walking or moving or anything, but I never passed out. Everything was kind of a blur because I was in shock.

They put me on a truck. I held onto my own leg, sitting on some guy's lap and bouncing along the road to the aid station. When I got there, the guy at the aid station gruffly told me to get up on the table, and they gave me a shot. Then the next thing I knew, I woke up in a cast with a pin through my leg. My left femur had been broken, and I was looking at a year for it to heal.

After that, I spent a day at the Air Force Base in Camh Ron Bay, four to five days at Clark Air Force Base in the Philippines, and three weeks in Japan before I got shipped to San Francisco. At Letterman Army Hospital in San Francisco, I was in an orthopedic ward, which is amputations basically. That was kind of tough for awhile because I had all my arms and legs and I knew I was going to be okay; I was just killing time while my leg healed. But there were guys there with one arm, one leg or two legs, one arm. Leg amputations were real common because there were a lot of mines in Viet Nam. It was more common to have a leg off than an arm.

The orthopedic ward was a little world unto itself. Everybody was in the same boat, so it wasn't that unusual to put your stump up on your tray. But then visiting days would come along. The men would want to see their families, but it would be kind of tough because people would come in with their eyes big around. Everybody else was used to everybody being in the same situation to one degree or another. But people would come in from the outside, and it would really be upsetting to see all these amputations. The guys would like to see people, but they'd sort of hate people coming in, staring and crying. It was pretty upsetting. Some of these people would come in to see their son and half of him would be gone. So when visiting day was over, there was a big sigh of relief and a feeling of "Let's get back to normal again." It was an interesting time.

Cpt. Philip G. Lenser

HMM 165, Marine Amphibian Unit : Vietnam

Phil Lenser: South China Sea—1975

From 1972 – 1977, it was my privilege to serve as a Marine officer and helicopter pilot. I flew the AH-1J "Cobra." The Cobra is the first helicopter created specifically for the attack role. The aircraft was designed to carry a whole array of ordnance but most typically we would outfit with guns and rockets. The full flex nose turret allows the pilot in the front seat to use his gun sight to aim the 20 mm, three barrel gatlin gun in nearly any direction, with every fourth round a tracer. Once the rounds started to flow, the stream could be directed to any target. The wing stubs, mounted to the fuselage, are platforms for the rocket pods. We carried 4 rocket pods with 19 rockets each for a total of 76 rockets. The rockets are 2.75" in diameter and about 4 feet in length and have a variety of warheads: high explosive, white phosphorus, or flachettes.

Helicopters fly by rotating airfoils overhead that create lift. The pitch of the rotor blades is controlled and varied by rods connecting them to a rotating disk called a swash plate that sits on top of the transmission. When the pilot moves the control stick in his right hand, the cyclic, the pitch is increased in the direction pointed, thereby causing the "pull" to move the aircraft that way. The lever in the left hand causes the bite of both blades to be increased or decreased, giving up and down movement. The rudder petals allow the pilot to change the pitch on the tail rotor to counterbalance the torque effect of the rotation of the main rotor. Helicopters don't naturally want to fly; hands off, they fall out of the sky. The best pilots have great skills and a delicate touch in using the flight controls to maneuver the aircraft.

Marine Corps helicopters are used to insert Marines into target areas or to assist in moving them from one location to another. Cobras are the close-in air support for these maneuvers or are used in defense of our ground forces. Working in pairs, a section of Cobras will work a target area, with the lead aircraft firing on the target in the first rocket run. As the lead comes off the target, the wing aircraft will roll in so that there is a continuous stream of ordnance on target.

During the evacuation of Saigon in 1975 Marine helicopters transported the last US forces and as many South Vietnamese supporters as possible from our embassy to the USS Hancock in the harbor.   I had just arrived at my overseas assignment and did not join the unit until 3 days after the completion of the extraction.

Here's part of what happened.   Our ambassador wanted to maximize the number of helpful Vietnamese we got out. He feared for their treatment under the advancing forces from the north.   The ship initially was relatively close to shore.   Those seeking refuge on the ship started using any means to get to sea and the safety of the US Navy.   Every type of watercraft headed out. Helicopters came from every corner, filling spots on the carrier to the point that they had to be pushed overboard to make room for the next. Some pilots even hovered over the sea, shut down and ditched their craft as they attempted to swim to the ship and make their escape. The carrier moved further to sea in an attempt to slow down the flow of craft. Our

Marine pilots were planning their time on station and fuel reserves based on the original location of the ship.

When the last helicopters left the embassy and headed to the ship the route was longer, the flight deck too clogged and the time in the air extended. Cobras land last; troops have priority, and it's always a good tactic to keep the guns on station at the ready the longest.

All but one made the deck. As luck would have it, the one that flamed out and ditched was the one that had a defective canopy explosive system. This system allows the pilot to blow the canopy to make escape on ditching a bit easier if the prospect of trying to swim free of a sinking mass of aircraft that you can't leave until the rotors stop spinning can be viewed as easy. Normally, the helicopter would not be flying with that system defective, but the mission meant all flyable aircraft go. So the crew chief had given the pilot a hammer. A hammer is better than a fist. Fortunately, the only loss was the aircraft. The hammer worked and our pilots were rescued and dry within short order.

The United States Marine Corps. The Corps. Grunt. Leatherneck. Jarhead. The few, the proud, the Marines.

There is nothing glamorous about war. There is something sacred about sacrifice, commitment, and shared misery. Watch bumpers of cars. The Marine Corps is the smallest branch of service, yet more Marine Corps emblems are worn on bumpers than any other service emblem. Why? Pride.

The change is forever. Once a Marine, always a Marine. Semper Fidelis.

Staff Sgt. Larry Mettler
11th Armored Calvary: Vietnam
Bronze Star, Purple Heart

Larry Mettler: Vietnam—1969

I was pretty old; I was 22 and drafted. At that time the draft was still on, and one could get a college deferment as long as one was in school. I finally graduated, and that was the end of that. In

January '68, pretty much everyone was getting drafted. There was still a big buildup in the late 60s, and so they were taking everyone who was eligible.

When we got drafted, we went in as privates. We went to the NCO school, and after that we came out as a sergeants. That was pretty cool. We might have the same stripes as some guy who'd been in the service for ten years. That kind of made some of the lifers pretty jealous. They used to call us "shake and bakes"—Shake and Bake Sergeants.

I jumped on at Travis Air Force Base and took the plane over. Pretty instant compared to some of the other folks in the past. We went over as individuals. When we got there, we had about a three-day orientation, then we were put on a helicopter and taken off to the bush and dropped off. They said "There's your vehicle and there's your three-man crew." So four days later, I was out in the bush.

Who were the men on my crew? I don't know. That's always a blank spot on my mind because I can remember their faces and all of the incidents, but I can't remember their names, which is really sad.

The crews on the armored personnel carriers (APCs) changed all the time because we worked as a team, but we went there as individuals. One guy might have two months left to serve, and another guy might have just arrived. Four people: the main .50 caliber machinegun, which was my position as turret commander, two .30 caliber side guns, and the driver. We lived in it all the time. Remember, we never went back. We got supplies every day by helicopter.

We were very mobile. That's what made us unique. Lots of times there would be an infantry patrol doing their job, and they'd get into trouble. So they would call the nearest armored group, and we would run over there and bail them out. The biggest threats to us were land mines and rocket-propelled grenades, which we hear about even today. We'd always want to drive behind the vehicles tracks in front of us, so we didn't blow up. If anyone was going to blow up, they were. I got out front more than I wanted to.

With all of the people that got wounded and injured, Medivac was pretty quick. That was probably why more people weren't killed. Combat still killed 58,000 people. People got killed standing next to you. I got wounded once. I didn't get a helicopter ride out 'til the next morning. I lay in a hospital bed for three days, got some stitches in my shoulder, and then I went back out.

There were never had enough people. I had guys in my unit who had three Purple Hearts already. Wounded three times and they were still out there fighting.

We got a new tank over there at the time called a Sheridan. It was like a heavy tank, but it wasn't an armored tank. I got one of those vehicles. It had a big main gun like a beehive round that fired little nails—little sharpened nails. It fired ten thousand nails with one shot. It was a pretty effective weapon. The nails would tear through jungle. They'd tear clothes off. They were pretty devastating.

Politics entered in before we even left home because nobody even wanted to go. I didn't know too many people who wanted to go. I was going to go for Navy aviation, but then I realized it was a six-year program. I was just getting out of college, and I said, "I'm not going to give you six years of my life."

Generally, we had the feeling that we were never really allowed to do what we could do to end the situation militarily. In general, we did our jobs, but we tried to stay alive and not be too heroic. My personal job was to stay alive and keep the guys with me alive. I wasn't as much concerned about the overall mission.

It's an individual thing, going from a war zone to civilian life. I've still got my memories. I really realize that the Viet Nam vets were for the most part mistreated. They were treated well in combat because they had all the supplies and all the facilities that they could get, mail call, and a quick response to medical needs plus only one year of duty.   But when they came home, nobody recognized that they did anything.

Sgt. Richard Pittman
5th Marines: Vietnam
Congressional Medal of Honor

Richard Pittman: Washington D.C.—May, 1968

In a four day period—July 21-24, 1966—
approximately a hundred and thirty of my friends
and Marines were killed and wounded.

We were just below the demilitarized zone on an operation called "Hastings" to try to lure the North Vietnamese into a certain area and then ambush them, kill them, capture them, do whatever. We were told we were going to move up to the highest point in the vicinity and become a radio relay station for artillery, airpower, etc. And so we started up a hill to this position. The company, about two hundred plus Marines, was moving in a column along a trail, and I was in the last squad in the column. Instead of going straight to the objective, the Commander at that time decided to take this well-used and open trail to the objective.

Everybody in the company was in that vicinity, and they were ambushed by North Vietnamese. Everybody was going to the front like we'd been told as Marines to do. I was following along. Our squad was definitely the last squad, but I didn't know where everyone was at that point because they were taking cover and then going down a trail.

By the time I got to the direction in which everyone was going, there was only one person sitting there. He had a machine gun between his legs, and there was some ammo sitting there. The only thing I remember about him was that he was a 3.5 rocket or anti-tank guy. I didn't see his anti-tanking weapon, but he had a machine gun, and I could hear all this firing and screaming and hollering that they needed more fire power. So I asked him if he was going to use the machine gun. I then took the gun and belted several rounds of ammunition together and took off down the trail.

As I was going down the trail, I came across North Vietnamese and shot whomever I could shoot at that time. Further down the trail, I came across wounded Marines and dead Marines. I just kept firing and maneuvering, trying to get up to the front because it appeared that I was the only machine gun firing at this time. And so when I got up to where the leading Marines were, it was kind of like the

Vietnamese and I got there at the same time. We were both surprised, and I just started shooting first.

There had actually been a little lull, and I didn't know how bad it had been up there. Later, I thought, well, it's just us reloading our magazines, our M-14s. When I got up there, I think the North Vietnamese were getting ready to make their final assault. I just started shooting. That's the only thing I can tell you. When my machine gun jammed, I picked up an AK-47 and kept firing until it ran out of ammunition. I then found a .45 caliber that belonged to another Marine. When my pistol ran out of ammo, I started throwing whatever grenades I could find. It's hard for people to understand, but training takes over and we do whatever comes naturally. I did what I was trained to do.

Medal of Honor Citation:

For conspicuous gallantry and intrepidity at the risk of his life above and beyond the call of duty. While Company 1 was conducting an operation along the axis of a narrow jungle trail, the leading company elements suffered numerous casualties when they suddenly came under heavy fire from a well concealed and numerically superior enemy force. Hearing the engaged marines' calls for more firepower, Sgt. Pittman quickly exchanged his rifle for a machinegun and several belts of ammunition, left the relative safety of his platoon, and unhesitatingly rushed forward to aid his comrades. Taken under intense enemy small-arms fire at point blank range during his advance, he returned the fire, silencing the enemy position. As Sgt. Pittman continued to forge forward to aid members of the leading platoon, he again came under heavy fire from 2 automatic weapons which he promptly destroyed. Learning that there were additional wounded marines 50 yards further along the trail, he braved a withering hail of enemy mortar and small-arms fire to continue onward. As he reached the position where the leading Marines had fallen, he was suddenly confronted with a bold frontal attack by 30 to 40 enemy. Totally disregarding his safety, he calmly established a position in the middle of the trail and raked the advancing enemy with devastating machinegun fire. His weapon rendered ineffective, he picked up an enemy submachine gun and, together with a pistol seized from a fallen comrade, continued his lethal fire until the enemy force had withdrawn. Having exhausted his ammunition except for a grenade, which he hurled at the enemy, he then rejoined his platoon. Sgt. Pittman's daring initiative, bold fighting spirit and selfless devotion to duty inflicted many enemy casualties, disrupted the enemy attack and saved the lives of many of his wounded comrades. His personal valor at grave risk to himself reflects the highest credit upon himself, the Marine Corps, and the U.S. Naval Service.

Sgt. Terry Quashnick
173rd Airborne: Vietnam
Bronze Star

Terry Quashnick: Vietnam—1969

We had a call that one of our reconnaissance teams on top of the mountain noticed a bunch of VC, all carrying AK's, moving into a village just before dusk. So, the lieutenant and the sergeant broke our company into three teams of four or five men to intercept these people, leaving one team behind to watch the base. Meanwhile, another team from one of our other logger sites was coming in from another direction, but they were much farther away and had a way to go yet.

As we came into the village, the two teams split up behind the hooches and we were going to peg them in. My team, or our lieutenant's team, intercepted them first. There were the sergeant, the RTO man, the lieutenant, another guy, and me at the end because I was the new guy and had been in country for about two months. The VC were coming through a field, walking toward our hooch and the other hooches. As they walked across the field, we came around the hooch and surprised them. The point man was trained to drop down to his knees and start firing, and the guy behind him was supposed to fire over the top of him.

Well, the lieutenant broke rank, ran around a

bullpen, and ran after them by himself because by that time they were all turning around and heading back. And I thought to myself, "He's alone. He's without cover." So I broke rank, ran behind the bullpen, and ran behind the lieutenant to cover him. I looked over to another hooch and there was a VC over there, so I raised my weapon toward him and opened fire; I just dumped the whole magazine. He took off around the hooch. Then the sergeant said, "Quashnick, get your ass on the ground!" So I dropped flat on the ground at that point, and the lieutenant kept right on running after those other guys.

The VC all disappeared. It was quiet. Finally, everybody came across the field. The wounded VC was gone and nobody knew where he went. We went over a hedge and over a ditch into another area. By this time, it was half an hour before being totally dark, so we decided to stay the night in that rice field. First, we tossed grenades into the ditch to make sure we were covered. Then we called in a chopper. The Huey came in thirty feet above our heads and used its mini-guns to rip the hedges up, completely mow them down. They had it pretty well secured for us to stay the night.

What bothers me is that in the middle of the night, I heard a guy holler from the area we had been earlier. So I crawled up to the lieutenant and said, "Lieutenant, I shot somebody over there, and I just heard him holler in that hooch." The lieutenant said, "Don't worry about it. We'll take care of it in the morning. We can't move anyone tonight." So, I crawled back to my spot on the ground and stayed there all night long.

The next morning we got up with the sunrise, and the lieutenant said, "Everybody pack up your stuff. We're moving back to base." I thought, I guess he doesn't want to check that guy out, so I let it go. Now, here's the real issue. When I got back to base, the E-6 sergeant and the E-5 sergeant came into my sandbag unit area, sat down, and said, "Terry, what the hell were you doing out there?"

I explained to the E-6 sergeant that I broke rank to protect the officer, the lieutenant, running across the field. He said, "You know what you did when you did that? You left our back exposed. What if they had gone around another way?" I said, "I wasn't thinking about that. All I was thinking about was saving the lieutenant's life." Then he said, "Next time a lieutenant wants to become captain and wants to do that crap, you let him do it on his own. You don't jeopardize the life of the whole group for one officer who wants to make rank."

I knew better and I apologized for it. The E-5 sergeant said, "We ought to put him in for a medal for this." My answer to that was, "I don't want a damn medal. The lieutenant's life, that's all I care about.

Cpl. Ruben Ramos
199th Light Infantry Brigade '68-'69: Vietnam
Two Purple Hearts

Ruben Ramos: Vietnam—February, 1969

We were in the jungle doing a three-company sweep on July 3, 1969. I was a machine gunner, and I also fired a cannon like a bazooka that shot a beehive round which is like little darts or metal arrows that go through any kind of trees, branches, vines, and so forth. We walked in on a battalion site's base camp of the Viet Cong. They were in the trees, they were in the ground, and everything. That firefight lasted that whole day.

I was firing my machine gun, when they called me up to the front to fire the cannon with the beehive round. There were only three of us who were authorized to fire them. So they brought us up to the front to fire these things. When we fired at the Viet Cong, they turned around and fired RPG's back, which are their rocket launchers. One of the rockets hit a big tree in front of me. You couldn't see daylight through the trees in the jungle, and the tree was coming down in my pathway. I started running, getting caught in vines and trying to get away out of the path of this tree, but the tree landed on me. I was temporarily paralyzed, knocked down, and unconscious.

When they finally got the tree off me, they

put me with the wounded. I wasn't wounded; I'd just had a tree fall on me. While I was there with the wounded, an RPG or a hand grenade landed there, and I got shot in my midsection. So, they Med Evac'd me that evening.

On July 4, I woke up in the hospital at Long Binh. The Donut Dollies, the Red Cross girls, came in, firing those little poppers filled with paper confetti to celebrate the Fourth of July. Well, I was shell-shocked and jumping all over the place.

To this day, I'm still shell-shocked. The thing is, I've learned to cope with things like that now, with lightning. The flash of light brings back flashes. A car backfiring, gun noises, take me right back to where we were. For a lot of years, I would hit the deck; I would hit the ground and cover my head.

Lt. Colonel Duane Saville

173rd Assault Helicopter Company: Vietnam
Bronze Star, Meritorious Service Medal

From 1967-1968, I was assigned as platoon Leader and later operations officer in the 173rd Assault Helicopter Company (Robinhoods) stationed in Lai Khe, Republic of Vietnam. In this unit, I flew a UH-1D Huey Lift helicopter, supporting various units: 1st Infantry Division, 25th Infantry Division, 199th Light Infantry Brigade, 101st Airborne Division, 173rd Infantry Brigade, Special Forces, Navy Seals, etc.

On November 30, 1967, I was out on a mission to support the 199th Light Infantry Brigade, located north of Ben Hoa RVN. At 1030 hours a call was received requesting a lift aircraft to proceed to Forward Support Base Concord to haul ammunition and smoke grenades to Alpha Company, which was in contact with the VC. In route, I monitored on the radio that Alpha Company was taking casualties and needed a dust-off immediately.

Diverting my aircraft to their position, I requested the tactical situation from the company commander (Heated Spotter 6). He advised me of the small arms and automatic weapons and to land on the south side of a group of trees to give my aircraft some cover from the enemy fire. There were two wounded soldiers on the riverbank and one severely wounded GI who had fallen off a steep, muddy twenty-foot river embankment into the Ben Hoa River after being shot. Cognizant of the many dangers involved, yet knowing that any delay could mean the loss of life, I proceeded into the landing zone with no helicopter light fire team available for cover.

The ground troops had started loading the two wounded soldiers on my helicopter when the VC opened fire. The third wounded soldier was still in the river and reportedly losing blood. The muddy riverbank kept caving in as troops tried to pull him out by a rope. Realizing the precarious situation of waiting to bring the individual up the bank with troops still in contact with VC, I suggested another solution—load the soldier from the river into the helicopter.

I pulled pitch and told the Commander that I would hover over the river and try to load the wounded soldier. I flew my chopper in an exposed-to-fire situation, making an approach into the river. I was able to set the skids under water and hold the aircraft belly at water level while hovering with the main rotor blade below the top of the bank. I then hovered sideways, bringing my main rotor blade to as close as six inches from the bank, with my pilot and door gunner's visual and verbal guidance. I was so close that the main blade was chopping leaves off of bushes on the side of the bank.

I kept the aircraft at this hovering position for at least three minutes while the crew chief swam out about five feet into the river to bring the wounded soldier to the chopper and load him in. The soldier was almost unconscious, having taken hits to the chest and the thigh. As soon as this last soldier was on board, I immediately took the wounded to the 93rd Hospital at Long Binh.

It was later on that I really realized the precarious situation I had been in and how lucky I was that nothing had happened to my crew or aircraft.

Sgt. Hugh "Bill" Snyder, Jr.
101st Airborne: Vietnam
Bronze Star, Purple Heart

Bill Snyder: Dong Tam, Vietnam—Sniper School—Feb., 1969

The funniest story occurred when I was squad leader at the time. We had a fellow who was our machine gunner, a young guy in his twenties, who

185

looked like Wally Cox with big, round glasses, red hair, big ears, short, just the typical kind of a cartoon character guy and about the neatest guy in the whole world.

We had moved into an area at dusk that was noted for a lot of hostility, and set up a defensive position by digging a large foxhole. When we dug a foxhole for four guys, it was pretty good size. We piled the dirt up in front, so we could hide behind the pile of dirt and put our machine gun on top of that. Well Marty, skinny as a rail, was our machine gunner. Now, if you think about that, it's kind of funny in itself because he carried more than what he weighed. But he was quite good at what he did.

We got set up for the evening and one of the other platoons moved out for an ambush type of setup right at dusk. There was a tree line about two hundred yards away, and they were going to move into the tree line to listen and watch because we'd heard that there was activity in there. So they were marching along and in the middle of all this, Marty had to go to the bathroom—number two. He went out, unbeknownst to us, in front of the foxhole behind a couple of bushes. While he was out there, one of the other guys and I went out to set up a booby trap flare type of thing about twenty-five to thirty feet away.

In the middle of all this, the platoon that was going out to the forest received incoming fire from the enemy. The natural reaction was to get back to the foxhole, the only safe place to. The other fellow that I was with was like 6'9" and took gigantic steps that I couldn't, but we finally made it up the hill to the foxhole.

We're so scared and trained to react so quickly that Marty felt that getting back to the foxhole was more important than pulling up his pants. So Marty came running toward the mound in front of the foxhole with his pants down, taking these little weird looking steps as if his legs were tied together. Well, when he got to the mound, because his pants were down around his legs, he couldn't take a large step. So he tripped over the mound and went head first into the hole. I and the other guy that I was with were watching the whole thing.

There were Marty's legs in the air, his pants still around his ankles, and toilet paper flying all over the place. And, believe me, if the enemy would have attacked at that particular time, we would have lost because we could not control our laughter.

Wesley E. Taylor
Marine Chief Engineer
Merchant Mariner:
WWII, Korea, Vietnam, Desert Storm

Throughout World War II, the United States Merchant Marine paid an exorbitant price to uphold their part of the war plan. One in 29 merchant mariners died in the line of duty, suffering a greater percentage of war-related deaths than the uniformed services. At least 8,651 were killed at sea and, conservatively 11,000 were wounded. Of the 11,000 wounded, 1,100 eventually died from the wounds, and 604 men and women were taken prisoner. Some were blown to death, some drowned, some froze, and some starved. Sixty died in prison camps. Of the 833 large ships sunk with millions of dollars of valuable cargo, 31 vanished with their mariner crews and Navy armed guard, without a trace into a watery grave.

One of the "unsung" heroes who served with the merchant marines was a young mid-Westerner, Wesley Taylor. Joining the maritime service in September, 1942, Wesley would continue to follow the mariner profession, sailing ships in peace and war. His final career years were spent working with the Department of Defense, on many programs vital to our defense posture. Wesley would eventually serve 46 years as a Marine Engineer and Chief Engineer. This is one of his many stories:

In 1973, while supporting operations in Vietnam, I was assigned a Chief Engineer on board the SGT Jack J. Pendleton (T-AK 276). Our mission was transporting ammunition to Vietnam and hauling retrograde ammunition and portable diesel generators from Da Nang, R.V.N. back to the United States. On the morning of September 21, 1973, the unthinkable happened. We ran aground, at full speed, on Triton Island, a reef, actually, which was a little bit of Chinese real estate in the South China Sea. Needless to say, running aground on Chinese real estate during the height of a war was not a good thing.

We dispatched a may day message and had surveillance air cover from Subic Bay, Philippines overhead in 20 minutes. The USS England, a Navy destroyer, came over the horizon to our rescue. They had dispatched their damage control team, by way of their work boat, and they were in route to assist us. While the work boar was in route, we received a message to not allow them on board, as the State Department needed to notify and confer with China regarding our circumstances. In due time, authorization was received to proceed with salvage activity. The USS Camden also arrived with Marine helicopters along with a sea going tug to assist in our rescue.

Leaving Da Nang the previous evening the ship was drawing 19 feet of water at the bow. My first act following the grounding was to have our damage control team take water depth soundings around the ship. The bow was now 17 feet <u>out of the</u>

water. The ship had hit the reef, shearing off coral heads as she came to a stop. The water was clear with many beautiful fish swimming around and the sky was also clear.

We were able to keep our power plant on line with engines available when we would need them to back off the reef. For the next seven to eight days, several attempts were made with tugs and operating the engines at extra full astern in an effort to free the ship. One could fry eggs on the engine casings. Yet, the ship clung tight to her chosen position.

This was also typhoon season in this part of the world, and we anxiously kept alert to the deteriorating weather reports. On the eight day, we were ordered to shut down and evacuate to the USS Camden. We had to leave the ship as a typhoon passed through. We were rescued off our ship via helicopter. While on board USS Camden, the captain and the crew were ordered back to our headquarters in Oakland except the First Mate, First Assistant Engineer, Chief Electrician, and me. We would work with the Navy to salvage the ship and cargo.

I was first up in the helicopter the next day to observe the status of the Jack J. Pendleton. It was obvious that there was considerable damage to the vessel in that the typhoon moved her down the beach, dragging anchors and coming to rest about a 1000 feet from her initial position.

Now the Chinese requested through the U.S. State Department that we remove the ship from their real estate. If unable to do so, it was decided that the Jack J. Pendleton be sunk in 180 feet of deep water.

As landing craft (LSTs) arrived to help us with the offload prior to scuttling the ship, we again became concerned with deteriorating weather conditions. Another typhoon was approaching with us as the bulls' eye target. Again, we had to evacuate the ship and return to USS Camden. After the typhoon passed, we once again got in the helicopter to survey the damage to our ship. The ship had now moved on to the reef and was figuratively speaking taking root. The open decks were a mess with broken cargo boons, the rudder was broken off, and the hull penetrated as a oil slick drifted away with the passing current.

We finished off loading the retrograde ammunition and a demolition team from New Orleans was flown in. There mission was to blow up part of the reef in order to permit the ship to sink. They failed as yet another typhoon was threatening. We removed the ship identification, name boards, etc. from the ship. The game plan was that the Navy would return the following February to sink the ship. After 46 days of being ship wrecked, I was finally on the way to the Philippines aboard one of the LSTs.

Over the years, I have wondered if the Pendleton would finally go to her grave at the bottom of the deep. Yet, it's my understanding that She is still there, stuck hard and fast.

Author's note: The Washington Post's Bob Woodward would later report that the Chinese and Vietnamese were at each other's throats just days after the Navy left; scavenging the wreckage.

2nd Class Petty Officer Dean "Fritz" Turner
Engineman
U.S.S. Brule: Vietnam

Fritz Turner: Bay of Vung Tau—Spring, 1967

It was easy to get to know the kids in Vietnam, and we always tried to do better by them. Sometimes upon arrival at Newport piers in Saigon, the ship would come under attack. Most of the time it was not serious, because no one was hurt, but it kept us on our toes.

One day, we were at Newport Piers, tied up and loading the ship. There were a bunch of us engineers on the fantail, the back of the ship, because the deck tech crew took care of most all the loading up there. There were about six of us back there, and Watch Landry was on watch. He was a shipfitter, and I never thought too much about this guy. I mean, we were all ship crewmembers, but he and I weren't very close.

We were sitting on davits and things, and all of a sudden these two kids, no more than 10 years old, in a native sampan or canoe boat, pulled up to the fantail of the ship. Landry swung down with his gun and placed them under arrest. I was thinking, "What's he doing with these two kids?" Lo and behold, that boat was full of grenades and C-4 explosives, and he had seen something. They could have taken us all out—taken the ship and all of us. At that quick glimpse, he saw something when there were six of us who didn't see a thing.

Over there, we didn't trust anybody. This would have been a mistake on our part, a very bad mistake.

PERSIAN GULF WAR

Lcpl. Marco Contreras
1st Marine Expeditionary Force
Operation "Desert Storm"

During Operations Desert Shield and Desert Storm, I was a 23 old year Lance Corporal (Lcpl.) E-3, with MASS-3, MACG-38, 3D MAW, (Marine Air Support Squadron 3, Marine Air Control Group 38, 3D Marine Aircraft Wing). My unit was called up in August as part of the 1MEF (1st Marine Expeditionary Force) to provide communications support for all Marine fixed and rotary wing elements. I was a field wireman, laying wire and operating the telephones and switchboards, working around the clock shifts—12 hours on and 12 hours off. I had joined the Marines because I wanted to challenge myself. I wasn't necessarily looking for combat, but I wanted to understand war firsthand.

It finally happened. When the air war commenced at 0238 Saudi time, January 17, or 6:38 p.m. EST January 16, the first of two air strikes went into effect. It wiped out their Air Force, elite Republican Guard, chemical and nuclear plants, and missiles aimed at Israel. While this went on, the first message from Baghdad was heard: "We will teach America and its allies a lesson." An Artillery BN (battalion) was scratched. We were informed that Iraqi tanks had surrendered to Israel. We lost one F-15 jet, maybe two others; the pilots didn't know yet. I couldn't believe how calm and relaxed we all were. I was asleep when the battle started, gave a radio check, then slept for two hours until 5:15 AM. I didn't know about it until I heard someone mention it 45 minutes later. My feeling at the time was so incredible. I was scared a little but happy because with the surprising low resistance, victory would come easily and we would go home sooner.

The next night, at approximately 11 p.m., I awoke to a combination of booms, which shook us and yanked us out of our zipped sleeping bags as if we were puppets on a string. Someone yelled, "Get in your holes!" and immediately there was chaos. Everyone was in a frantic rush looking for MOPP gear, rifles, and flack jackets. I remember very distinctly Cpl. Spear yelling, "Where is my gas mask?"

Cpl. Jackson came in from the SB (switch board tent), threw aside a cot, and ripped open a covering to expose the 5ft x 5ft hole we had dug in our tent. Everyone gathered his stuff, standing ready to jump in. Shaking, I moved apprehensively around the hole. We all hesitated, looking at each other before we jumped in. In the hole were Cpl. Jackson, Cpl. Irwin, Sgt. Sinclaire, Lcpl. Martin, and myself, along with two packs which were at the bottom of our feet, various MOPP gear, and our gas masks in our hands, soon to cover our faces, a feeling of crampedness, close quarters, and discomfort was in the air. We talked about how we should have made the hole bigger. The reserve sergeant from New Jersey was very scared and started to cry. He had only joined the Marine

Reserves to qualify for a home loan. His crying was bad for our morale and a poor example of leadership. I began to question people who had joined the military for the wrong reasons. A short time later, Gunny Ring came by and said a few rockets were launched towards the Northeastern border but did no apparent damage. We stayed in that hole with gas masks on, silent, listening for the next alarm, the dreaded one alerting us to put on our MOPP gear.

At roughly 1000, during the time I was on SB watch, a blast was heard near the road. Martin and Sinclaire rushed from their sleep to put on their boots, and I ran out to the bunker thinking it was an Iraqi T-72 tank. I was positive it was a tank. A short time later, Lt. Griggs called from the Ops tent and informed us it was a misfire from a Moroccan antiaircraft gun. What I didn't understand is why it was so close. I questioned whether the Moroccans could be trusted. Sometime later Lcpl. Murray, our arms rep., walked in and asked to be patched over to the Guard Chief. Very seriously, Murray told the SSgt. about the Moroccans laying communications wire near the fence. I told him it was reported this morning. He said dramatically, "It's not like we are back in Pendleton, that we have to inspect everything." He also said, "Those Moroccans could very easily not be Moroccans, but Iraqis posing as Moroccans. I'm 20 now and I want to live to be 21."

Two weeks later, we were on the move again. The move reminded me of a school field trip, only this one was in a time of war.

OPERATION RESTORE HOPE
(SOMALIA)

Major John "Jeff" Williamson
9th Marines: Operation "Restore Hope"
Meritorious Service Medal

Jeff Williamson: Veterans' Day—2003

By December of 1992, the situation in Somalia had degraded so that within twelve months an estimated one million people were expected to die of starvation and the ensuing civil war. Already on a six month western Pacific (Westpac) deployment in the Indian Ocean, my battalion, the 2nd Battalion of the 9th Marine Regiment (2/9) was ordered to Somalia to secure and stabilize the capital city of Mogadishu. The battalion was to conduct the first combat amphibious landing since Korea, more than 50 years earlier.

My platoon's mission was to seize the international terminal complex and tower at the Mogadishu International Airport so that the airfield could be used to bring in humanitarian relief supplies and follow-on forces. This would be done by landing across the beach adjacent to the main runway, by capturing the tower and all the hangars, and by destroying any enemy forces that resisted the landing.

We were going to land, in darkness, in ten amphibious assault vehicles (AAVs). These are lightly armored, tracked personnel carriers capable of launching from naval ships and carrying fifteen to twenty Marines each to the shore via propellers in the water and tracked tank-like treads once on the shore. At the time, I was a second lieutenant, not more than nine months out of the Infantry Officer Course in Quantico, and I was commanding my very first platoon...and taking them into combat!

We launched from the U.S.S. Juneau at 0300 on 10 December 1992, and as soon as we hit the water, all the communication gear went out in my AAV, so I couldn't talk to any of my other vehicles. I was in the commander's hatch of the lead AAV, with a squad of thirteen Marines, and one reporter in the back, and I couldn't talk to anybody! After five minutes of bobbing in the ocean in the dark and trying to fix the comm, I visually waved the next AAV towards the beach, which was about a mile away. This hand-and-arm signal was passed to the other nine AAVs, and we started towards the landing site.

The intelligence brief, which we received on the ship, indicated that there were an estimated six hundred armed Somalis who would potentially be defending the airfield and attempting to disrupt the landing. So now we were about one half of the way to the beach, and I was starting to feel very excited and nervous. Just as I began to make out the shoreline, the propellers in my AAV and one other just stopped working. (One thing that the Marine Corps has taught me is that whenever you think you've solved one problem, another presents itself.) The only thing one can do when this happens is to engage the tracks and use the tank treads like paddles. So my AAV and one other were under track-propulsion and drifting south in the current while the other eight AAVs were still moving quickly toward the beach.

By the time we hit the shore, we were about a mile south of our landing spot and the rest of my platoon. I still couldn't talk to them but was assuming that they were up on the main beach making the landing. All of a sudden, off in the distance to the north, I saw all these bright flashes of light.

The main weapon system on an AAV is a Mark-19 grenade launcher. It's a machine gun that literally throws grenades out, and the resulting explosions look remarkably like lots of little flashes off in the distance. Still not able to talk to my platoon, I was convinced that my Marines were just getting hammered on the beach. I was thinking that they were engaged in heavy combat at the landing zone and that their platoon commander was nowhere near them!

"We've got to get up there!" I screamed over the headset intercom. As you can imagine, I was a pretty young guy, new and relatively inexperienced, going into combat for the first time of my life, and the conflicted feelings that I had were amazing. I thought, "Wow, I've got to get into the fight, right now!" and, "Wow, I'm really lucky I'm not on that beach right now 'cause they're getting pounded." It's like I was happy and not happy at the same time.

So my two AAVs came tearing up along the beach towards our landing zone to try and flank the enemy from the south. As we crested one of the sand dunes, we just about crushed a huge group of reporters who were assembled in the dark along the beach, taking pictures of the Marines' landing.

The self-restraint from the young gunners on board the AAVs was amazing. They saw a bunch of people in the dark, and must have been thinking the same thing that I was about the reported enemy. They could have just opened up on all these people and killed them. They didn't. It must have taken Herculean self-restraint not to fire as the reporters' flash photography began right in front of them in the dark. It didn't take long to realize that these were the flashes I had seen off in the distance!

We all quickly recovered from the initial shock of meeting the phalanx of media, took a hard left, and headed across the runway. We linked up with the rest of the platoon and accomplished our mission, with no one the wiser about all the problems we had had on the landing. All that the international reporters reported, and the rest of the world saw on television, was a perfect Marine amphibious landing, with a tactically sound flanking movement to boot!

Editor's note: 2nd Lt Williamson's platoon remained in Somalia with the 15th Marine Expeditionary Unit, Special Operations Capable (15th MEUSOC), for another two months. They conducted another "textbook" amphibious landing under enemy fire in the southern city of Kisamayu, and led numerous raids and patrols against Somali enemy positions. They returned to the United States on 15 April 1993.

Sgt. Magdy J. Zakhary
Marine Corps: Operation "Restore Hope"

Somalia is on the easternmost tip of the African continent and a few degrees above the equatorial line. By February of 1992 the United States and the world had seen enough bloodshed in this country and had, some say reluctantly, decided to act. I was part of a U.S. Marine Corps detachment assigned to the United Nations. We were being sent to bring "peace" to this little sliver of inhumanity and to stop the death of the "innocents", if there ever was such a group. We were there to try and stymie the flow of blood created by the feuding factions. When we first arrived we were cheered and welcomed with open arms and applause by citizens of this country. That would all quickly change for the worse. I have no way of knowing what the powers that be were thinking when they sent us, America's sons and daughters, over there to that God-forsaken place.

Perhaps the people in the United Nations thought that they could finally get one right. They had screwed up everywhere else thus far: Beirut, the Congo and Iraq in the post- Gulf War times. We were told this time was supposed to be different, so they sent us in. I remember my friends and I, sitting in the worst place we had ever been, start wondering how long before the cheering and applause would be replaced by bullets and bloodshed. Fortunately, we would not have to wait too long to find out.

The climate was crippling to us. The very air we were breathing was thick and acrid. The humidity made us feel as though we had just stepped out of the sauna or that someone was standing over us with a hose continuously dousing us with water. A few weeks earlier we had been enjoying ourselves without a care in the world, a bunch of young Marines enjoying the tropic like breeze on the beaches of San Diego. Now we were in this indescribable place.

If you've ever seen the movie *Saving Private*

Ryan with Tom Hanks or *Mad Max* with Mel Gibson, you'll have a basis to form a mental picture of what I'm about to describe. If you never have seen a realistic war movie then try and imagine a city in total anarchy. There is no law or rules whatsoever: people killing one another for a spoonful of food and parents selling their kids for a few dollars.

As with any war or conflict the very young and the very old or ill always pay a disproportionate price. This place was no different. The emaciated, starved bodies of the elderly and young littered the streets. A pickup truck from the United Nations went around town picking up the bodies twice a day: nine in the morning and four in the afternoon. The driver did his job rather unceremoniously. With as much emotion and thought as you or I would put into taking out the trash or flushing the toilet, the driver would grab the bodies and throw them into the bed of the truck. The driver could grab most of the bodies with one hand. They were so light. He would grab the kids, infants or babies by an arm or a leg; sometimes the driver would just grab a handful of hair and with a flick of his wrist the bodies would go sailing in the air. I remember the bodies landing in a heap in the bed of the truck. When they started to cone at the top the driver would grab a rake or shovel and level off the mound. Human beings had no value here, dead or alive. Any semblance of order, civility or humanity was long gone.

Try and imagine your worst nightmares of how uncaring and uncompassionate mankind can sometimes be to one another. When you have this mental picture painted vividly in your mind, realize you haven't even come close to this reality. The strong and the powerful, without remorse, devour the weak, sometimes for their own gain and sometimes out of shear boredom, for nothing more than their own amusement. There is nothing else for them to do—these thugs with guns, many of whom are no older than fourteen or fifteen—so they torment the weak.

Every building and street, every corner and alley was torn apart by this civil war. There was not one building that remained wholly intact or untouched. The pavement in the streets had been dug up and the water pipes ripped out from the ground. It was impossible to make a phone call because the telephone wires had been ripped down off of the phone poles; eventually the telephone poles themselves even disappeared. The fixtures, windows, doors, furnishings and even the carpeting and baseboards had been removed from virtually every building we ever walked into. Anything that was or possibly could be of any value had been taken away. This was the worst destruction I have ever seen in my life, even more devastating and destructive than the aftermath of the attacks on the Twin Towers on September 11, 2001. This is how I remember Somalia. It was a living nightmare. For some I'm sure it still is.

It was about noontime and we were trudging through the streets of Mogadishu on yet another fruitless and time consuming "sweep" of the city's ghettos. We all had to wear our flak jackets . There we were in the middle of the desert, sand and dust and mud huts all around us, and we were totally dressed in green. It was par for the course. On this patrol Sergeant Washington was on point. Usually I would have been but since this was new territory for us and we didn't quite have our routine down, Sgt. Washington took point, guiding us through the maze of the ghetto.

Sgt. Washington and I had both served in the Gulf War and took part in the battle of Khafji. I was older than he was, but he was my superior. He earned his position as well as my respect, and we worked very well together. We knew each other's body language and moods. It was like we could almost read each other's minds. There were seven other Marines in our unit, nine in all. It might seem like a small sized element given our location and mission but we were well trained, motivated, battle tested and ready. Not to mention the fact that most of the weight on our backs was comprised of claymore mines, grenades, ammunition for our rifles and a host of other goodies. My perception of why we were here and what I thought of these people and this place was about to change.

The ghetto we were patrolling in was about three hundred meters behind the former five-star hotel, the Al-Sahafi. We were about a quarter mile from the nearest American unit, which was patrolling on a parallel course to our northeast. The ghetto was the most unimaginable and unbelievable living environment I had ever seen—no running water or toilets. People relieved themselves in cans or buckets; sometimes they did their business right were they stood. We were walking in human waste, nothing less than an open sewer and the smell was indescribable. There was no electricity, which meant no refrigeration of any kind. That didn't matter much because no one had any food.

Everybody was starving to death. The average shelter was nothing more than cardboard and tin siding slapped together haphazardly with bailing wire or rolls and rolls of tape. I recall thinking that the poorest in America would be millionaires here.

As we were walking, a fight of some sort broke out between two Somali men. They were about sixty feet in front of us. One man looked fifty years old. He was wearing a torn and frayed white dress shirt that had huge butterfly collars, lime green corduroy pants and tennis shoes. His shirt was buttoned all the way to the top. The second man seemed to be about twenty years old. He had on a white Nike T-shirt with a silhouette of Michael Jordan in mid-air, just about to dunk a basketball. He was wearing a pair of red slacks and brown sandals. Something about the situation put me on edge; it just didn't seem right. I couldn't quite figure out what it was.

Sgt. Washington was in the front, I was directly behind him, and the rest of the patrol was behind me. Corporal Kruger was in the back. Corporal Kruger was new to the unit, and I didn't know him too well. He was also a Gulf War veteran and had seen some action in Kuwait. He was a big strapping jock type from Nebraska. The kind of guy you just knew played football. He had no neck and arms the size of an average man's thighs. An intimidating looking fellow in jeans and a T-shirt, let alone in full combat gear with grenades tied to his body.

I was on the radio trying to relay our current position and situation to our sister unit a few hundred meters away. I looked back at Corporal Kruger and the rest of my unit and realized we were in trouble. The reason I had that uneasy, gnawing feeling about the fight in front of us became frighteningly clear. The two men seemed to be fighting but were really not. There was no bloodshed, no telltale signs of a struggle, no angry crowd gathered around the two, taking sides and cheering on a favorite. The two Somali men were putting on a show. They were trying to draw us in and set us up; they had succeeded. We had walked straight into an ambush.

Try and imagine a huge "V" shape that is about 75 yards long from end to end. We had walked in from the open end and were about three-quarters of the way through. This is what's described in the military as the "fatal funnel," the reason being is simple. Anyone caught in the position we were currently in would usually suffer fatal results. The "V" shape creates a situation similar to that of a bottleneck, and it's probably one of the best ambush techniques known. It is simple to do and hard to detect. If we were to get pinned down it would be extremely difficult for us to fight our way out of.

As I turned back towards Sgt. Washington, I could tell that he also had just realized we were walking into an ambush. He had turned his head to look back at me and I could see it in his eyes and body language. At that instant, the wall of the hut in front of us was ripped to shreds by machine gun fire. Someone on the inside had let loose with a large burst and the bullets had torn apart the wall. Simultaneously we both yelled "Ambush!" and dropped down flat on our bellies. The other seven Marines did the same, and we all were rolling around in human waste.

Corporal Kruger was facing the way we had just come from. He was trying to prevent some Somali gunmen from taking up positions against us.

In a situation like this everything slows down and speeds up at the same time. Everyone reacts without thinking or being told. It's reflex. Whole sentences or even paragraphs of communication are reduced to one or two words and a gesture or posture of one's body. "Ammo," "Como," "Rear Flank": phrases which probably mean nothing to the uninitiated mean everything to those who know and have been tested.

So there we were, nine Marines, all of us covered in human feces, urine and mud. Bullets were flying at us from every direction and we were returning fire in every direction. I remember thinking, "Why are we here trying to help these people?" This wasn't Vietnam. We had the support and backing of the American people, the United Nations, and the world. We were the good guys, patrolling this ghetto to keep its inhabitants safe from the armed thugs that had been terrorizing this country. The same hoodlums that had pillaged, raped and destroyed this city and the whole country were now being helped by there former "victims". The people we were trying to protect had turned on us and were trying to kill us. I was starting to get a little mad.

Sgt. Washington grabbed my arm and yelled in my ear "We gotta move now or we are dead!" I looked back at Corporal Kruger's position and saw four other Marines helping him. I also saw something that made me freeze for a few seconds. The Somalis shooting at us were not men but boys—I mean eight, nine or ten years old maximum. Sure there were men in the crowd, but most of the shooters looked no older than twelve. There were even a few women. All told I estimated a crowd of about one hundred people to our rear and about thirty to our front. We were badly out numbered.

Over the radio I heard that our sister unit was on the way to help, helicopters were in the air heading towards us and fighter jets had been scrambled to come help us. I yelled at Sgt. Washington, "Give me your two claymores!"

Sgt. Washington and the two remaining Marines were firing off there rounds as fast as they could pull the trigger on their rifles. The smell of cordite and gunpowder was in the air. Sometimes when I take a deep breath I still have a sense of the intoxicating feeling I got from the combination of cordite, human feces and fear. It is a memory burned in my mind.

I remember trying to make an improvised high explosive charge with Sgt. Washington's two claymores as well as two of my own. The tape kept slipping out of my hands as I was straining to wrap all four claymores into one big bundle. I kept fumbling with the roll for what seemed like an eternity. I knew if I could make my device work, we would experience a comparable level of ecstasy. When I finally got it situated the way I wanted, I ended up with what looked like four VCR tapes stacked together.

Each claymore has the equivalent of about two sticks of dynamite as well as over 900 bullets in each. I had just created an explosive device with a total combined power of over eight sticks of dynamite and more than 3600 bullets in a single punch. All I had to do was get it close enough to the crowd.

I sloshed through the mud and the muck to where Sgt. Washington was positioned. He and the other two Marines with him were putting out an enormous amount of firepower. I yelled at him to

"Watch the bouncing ball!" holding up my little creation and then handed him the detonator.

The crowd at Corporal Kruger's end was being held off but just barely. They were the issue of my greatest concern. As I stood up and started running towards them I heard Sgt. Washington's booming voice yell "Covering fire!"; he was trying to give me some protection.

I ran about ten or fifteen yards and threw my "baby" into the air with all my might. It landed with a thud and flipped end over end a few times and stopped about thirty yards away from the crowd. As soon as the claymore stopped rolling, Sgt. Washington pressed the button on the detonator.

The sound was deafening. It was as if someone had tied my head to the engine of a 747 jumbo jet as it struggled to break the bonds of gravity on take-off. The shockwave knocked me on my back, and I almost dropped my rifle. I remember the crowd simply disappearing, as if they had been vaporized. At least half of them lay there dead.

If you have ever watched a movie where a real suspenseful part is played in slow motion that's what this was like. Every detail, no matter how small, is forever caught in my mind. I can still see the plastic covering of the claymores flying through the air. I can see the projectiles, the bullets, as they fly in the air. I see the bodies being lifted up off the ground from the force of half a dozen bullets tearing into there flesh all at once; they look like rag dolls being tossed around. Some bodies drop to the ground like a sack of potatoes.

The rest of the people shooting at us stopped. They dropped their weapons and took off running in all different directions with their hands in the air. This would be the strongest show of force the Marines would ever have to display while in Somalia.

The whole thing from start to finish lasted less than ninety seconds. I have no regrets or remorse for the actions of me and my Marines that afternoon. We did what we had too. We suffered two wounded Marines and killed fifty-eight enemy. We were able to come home and keep on living.

The lesson I learned during my time in Somalia was not to be unappreciative or take for granted what I have. America's not heaven, but I think it's the closest thing on Earth.

Editor's Note: The above story was written by the author himself.

OPERATION IRAQI FREEDOM

Major John "Jeff" Williamson
23rd Marine Regiment: Operation "Iraqi Freedom"
Meritorious Service Medal

Jeff Williamson: An Nasiriyah—March, 2003

My worst day of the war. It was the March 25, 2003. My company had crossed the

Kuwaiti/Iraqi border four days earlier and had been traveling 24 hours a day since. We had fought through our first major combat the day prior in An Nasiriyah, where the regiment had taken heavy losses. I hadn't slept but an hour or two per day in the last five days and was starting to feel the effects of both the sleep deprivation and the continuing stress.

The entire regiment was moving north along a two-lane north-south road, with our battalion about one-third of the way back in the regimental column. There were hundreds of vehicles all trying to get up this road, so you can imagine the difficulty getting anywhere if you weren't the lead vehicle. In this part of Iraq, the terrain is largely marshland, so off-road mobility was not possible. If the convoy stopped for any reason, we ended up pulling alongside the road and having to wait, exposed on both flanks to enemy attack, until the column started moving again.

As we approached Al Gharraf, just north of An Nasiriyah, we were fragged (given a fragmentation order from the regiment) to assist an artillery battery of the 11th Marines. They had been ambushed, some of their Marines wounded, and they were pinned down on the northern side of the town. We were tasked with attacking the enemy in Al Gharraf in order to relieve the pressure on this artillery unit and allow them to pull back into friendly lines and reach medical attention.

So my company and one other dismounted the vehicles, moved by foot, and attacked into the southern part of the town, driving the enemy force out. About the time we were consolidating in the town, it started getting real dark and dusty—the beginning of a fierce sandstorm that would ultimately stop the regiment in its tracks. The storm significantly cut down visibility, and we started getting shot at sporadically from all different directions. The "Fedayeen Saddam" fighters were taking advantage of the low visibility to come up to the edge of the column, shoot a little, and bounce back out into the darkness again.

In the process of taking the town, the battalion took multiple prisoners of war, many of them severely wounded. My company was tasked to assign one platoon to watch these and other POWs that the regiment had taken (about one hundred in total), while the rest of the company moved about five miles north of town to establish a defensive blocking position in order to keep the enemy from coming south down the road. So I put a platoon of about thirty Marines watching the POWs and took the other two platoons up north to set in.

We had been told there would be other units to link up with, but when we arrived, we found absolutely no one. We were the furthest unit north in the whole regiment and completely alone. As we tried to establish our defensive positions (in near total darkness, with no air-support, and completely alone), we got ambushed again. I made the decision to return to friendly lines.

When we finally made it back to the town, it took me hours to find my other platoon in the dead of night with the sandstorm blowing around, driving rain, and thousands of vehicles and Marines strewn all over the place. Finally, I found them, and we all collapsed alongside our vehicles. I was exhausted and absolutely needed to sleep. I told my executive officer, "You need to take charge because I'm going to do something to get people killed if I don't get some sleep right now." So I just lay down to sleep in a mud puddle.

I was wet, cold, had sand blowing in my face, and all these POWs were screaming because half of them were wounded. We were on the front lines, and there was not a lot of medical support and doctors to go around, so these POWs were making a hell of a racket. I'd finally gotten in my sleeping bag because it had gotten so cold, and was sleeping with my pistol on my chest.

The whole night was absolute chaos! The artillery units right next to us were hammering away all night long, each "boom" shaking the ground and making me jump and wonder if it was incoming or outgoing. Sporadic small-arms fire was heard from just about all directions, and the sand and rain kept coming. I was awakened at some point by a strange sound, and managed to roll over and put on my night vision goggles in time to see this legless guy dragging himself right next to me. I just basically yelled, "Guard, guard, get over here and get this guy!" Two Marines ran over, saying "Sorry, sir," picked him up and carried him back to the POW area.

It was hell, and it was probably the best night's sleep in my whole life. It was the only time in the whole war, and probably in my whole career, where I just went, "This is just too much for me. I can't do this. How the hell do I get out of here?"